INFORMATION
AND
MISINFORMATION

INFORMATION AND MISINFORMATION

An Investigation of the Notions
of Information, Misinformation,
Informing, and Misinforming

CHRISTOPHER JOHN FOX

CONTRIBUTIONS IN LIBRARIANSHIP AND
INFORMATION SCIENCE, NUMBER 45

GREENWOOD PRESS
Westport, Connecticut • London, England

Library of Congress Cataloging in Publication Data

Fox, Christopher John.
  Information and misinformation.

  (Contributions in librarianship and information
science, ISSN 0084-9243 ; no. 45)
  Bibliography: p.
  Includes index.
  1. Information science—Philosophy. 2. Communication
—Philosophy. I. Title. II. Series.
Z665.F76 1983   020'.1   83-5545
ISBN 0-313-23928-2 (lib. bdg.)

Library of Congress Catalog Card Number: 83-5545
ISBN: 0-313-23928-2
ISSN: 0084-9243

First published in 1983

Greenwood Press
A division of Congressional Information Service, Inc.
88 Post Road West
Westport, Connecticut 06881

Printed in the United States of America
10 9 8 7 6 5 4 3 2 1

To my parents

CONTENTS

ACKNOWLEDGMENTS

I am indebted to a great many people for their help and encouragement throughout the two-year period during which this essay was written. I am especially grateful to two individuals who made enormous contributions of time, energy, and ideas. Leigh Estabrook was the first to suggest that I develop my early notions on the nature of information into a coherent and detailed position. She read every draft of the manuscript and made innumerable suggestions for improving and refining it. Rich Hall was my main source of guidance concerning the philosophical topics discussed in the book, which of course amounts to most of it. If not for the frequent discussions and detailed readings of many versions of the manuscript that he provided, this book would be much less successful in achieving its goals than it is.

I am also grateful to the many people who read one or another (or several) versions of the manuscript and made helpful comments and criticisms, especially Jonathan Bennett, Evelyn Daniel, Bill Frakes, Jeff Katzer, Bob Oddy, and Bob Taylor. These people also made vital contributions by discussing various points of my position with me, as did many others, including Barbara Abbott, Susan Blood, Beth Carley, Gene Cline, Paul Gandel, Herb Hendry, and Rich Veith.

I wish to thank Berta Segretti and Gina Chang for rapidly putting my handwritten manuscript into machine-readable form, and Diane Crowe and Linda Meek for typing various reworked portions of the manuscript.

Finally, I wish to thank Judy Mardigian for her constant encouragement of, and endless patience with, an irritable and frequently disgruntled housemate. The stable and comfortable environment she was instrumental in providing contributed enormously to the completion of this work.

All errors, omissions, and shortcomings of my position are, of course, my own.

INFORMATION
AND
MISINFORMATION

1

INTRODUCTION

1.1 SCOPE OF THIS STUDY

Information seems to be everywhere. We talk of its being encoded in the genes, so it must be carried in every living cell of every living thing. We say that it is disseminated by media of communication, so it must be transmitted around the world by wire, microwave, laser light, and radio wave, broadcast by television and radio, and printed in newspapers, magazines, journals, and so on. We say that information is exchanged in conversation, so it must be present in billions of the utterances occurring every day. Information is also said to be contained in all sorts of things, including books, letters, telegrams, films, tapes, computers, and minds. A large segment of the population is said to be employed in "information-related occupations" in a wide range of industries, and a large and growing industry is itself exclusively devoted to the tasks of storing, retrieving, processing, transmitting, and disseminating information. A science is devoted to the study of information. Libraries are overflowing with it, institutions are bogged down by it, and people are overloaded with it.

Information, then, is as ubiquitous as air, or heat, or water. But it differs from these latter things in having a far more mysterious nature. For although we can say quite exactly what air, heat, and water are, no one seems to know exactly what information is.

This is not to say that no attempt has been made to provide a definition of 'information'. The literature of information science is rife with such attempts, and several disciplines (like statistics and information theory, for example) have adopted definitions of 'information' that have proven useful for their purposes. The difficulty is rather that despite such attempts, no one has yet come up with an analysis of 'information' that adequately captures what is meant by the term when it is used in the sorts of contexts alluded to in the first paragraph above. The various discipline-specific characterizations of information (like those of information theory and statistics) fall short of this goal by excluding from consideration various important features of information not needed for their specific purposes. On the other hand, information scientists have simply failed to supply an adequate analysis of the notion of information, despite the best efforts of many researchers over many years (see Chapter 3 for support of this claim). As a result, information science is in the rather embarrassing position of lacking any clear understanding of its central notion, and science in general is likewise without an adequate account of an entity which, as pointed out above, seems to turn up everywhere.

In this study I take the first steps toward rectifying this situation by providing an analysis of the notion of information and the related concepts of misinformation, informing, and misinforming. This work is intended primarily as a contribution to the foundations of information science, so special attention is given to the literature and concerns of this field. However, since conceptual analysis is fundamentally a philosophical activity, the method I employ is that of contemporary analytic philosophy. The remainder of this chapter is devoted to specifying in greater detail the aims of this study and to explaining and defending the method employed to achieve them.

1.1.1 The Ordinary Notion of Information

It was noted above that various disciplines have adopted the term 'information' for their own purposes, giving it a precise definition and using it in a special way. Even though this sort of stipulative characterization of information is in principle quite arbitrary, it is almost always the case that such special uses of the term 'information' are very closely related to the uses of this term in ordinary language. This is probably explained by the fact that when an established term like 'information' is used in a special way, it is expected that this special use is somehow akin to the established use. Otherwise, there is every reason to prefer an entirely new term to the old established term. In short, we expect that the various discipline-specific uses of 'information' have a reasonably strong connection to the ordinary use of the word. It is clear that this requirement is generally recognized, since it is typically the case that when a discipline-specific definition of 'information' is introduced, a point is made of appealing to our intuitions about the ordinary use of the word to justify various features of the definition. Discussions of information by information theorists (Jones [1979], for example) usually provide good illustrations of this point. Information theorists typically argue in favor of their definition of 'information' by appealing to our intuitions about the ordinary use of 'information' in "quantitative" contexts in which we say there is "more" or "less" information present.

One standard against which any proposal regarding a definition of 'information' must be evaluated, then, is the ordinary use of the word. Consequently, it seems that an investigation of the notion of information must begin, at least, with the ordinary language notion of information.

There is, however, a more compelling reason for providing an analysis of the ordinary notion of information in the course of explicating the concept of information at work in information science: the notion of information in information science is substantially *identical* with the ordinary notion of information.

There are two arguments in support of this claim. First, information scientists have not at all succeeded in articulating a theory or definition of 'information' acceptable to a majority of researchers in the field (this fact is documented in Chapter 3). There is no discipline-specific characterization of information in information science as there is in statistics and information theory. Nevertheless, information scientists apparently do succeed in communicating with one another quite effectively regarding information and related concepts. Such communication must be based on some common notion of information, and the only likely candidate seems to be the ordinary notion of information. Indeed, given that no more than a handful of information scientists can be found in support of any one of the score or so proffered definitions of 'information' in the information science literature, there doesn't seem to be any other way to explain how information scientists can succeed in making themselves understood to one another and to the scientific community as a whole. Thus the ordinary notion of information, as the notion that supports communication about information among information scientists, must in fact be the notion of information that delineates the focus of study in information science.

The second reason for supposing that 'information' is used in its ordinary sense in information science is based on the verbal practice of information scientists. Except for occasional malapropisms (that tend to occur in discussions of information, and usually under the influence of the author's opinions on this topic), the use of this word in the literature of information science appears to conform entirely to ordinary use. Hence there is no reason, given the literature of the field, to suppose that 'information' is used in any but its ordinary sense by information scientists.

I conclude, then, that an investigation of the notion of information in information science must begin with, and furthermore really amounts to, an investigation of the ordinary notion of information. The same arguments, and the same conclusions, apply regarding the other concepts I wish to consider in this study, namely the notions of misinformation, informing, and misinforming.

Of course, this does not mean that the ordinary notions of information, misinformation, informing, and misinforming must turn out, upon investigation, to be perfectly suited to the purposes of scientific inquiry. On the contrary, it may turn out that these ordinary notions are quite unsuitable for these purposes. If so, then careful study may lead to recommendations for changing these notions to make them more serviceable as tools of information science. No such recommendations, however, are made in this essay. Rather, attention is restricted to the logically prior task of carrying out a detailed examination of these notions as they are currently understood among information scientists.

1.1.2 Carriers of Information

Having broadly defined the scope of this investigation to be the analysis of the ordinary notion of information, several restrictions of this scope must be noted. The first has to do with carriers of information. (Throughout this essay, I use the term 'carry' as a theoretically neutral means of referring to the relationship between information and those things with which it is somehow associated.) Information is commonly spoken of as being carried by a very wide range of entities, including pictures, drawings, photographs, plans, blueprints and graphs, spoken and written languages, gestures, hand signals and other non-verbal behavior, genes and DNA, electro-magnetic and sound waves, mechanical and electro-mechanical devices, records, tapes, films, holographs and video-disks, and so on. Although ultimately a theory of information must make sense of the ways all these entities carry information, it greatly simplifies the early stages of theory development to focus attention on information carried by just a few kinds of things. In this work I deal *only* with information carried by sentences.

There are three reasons for focusing particularly on information carried by sentences. First, language is arguably both the central and the most important means of conveying information. Many of the carriers of information listed above can be construed as instances of symbols of a language or carry information by virtue of the fact that they can be mapped into instances of symbols of a language. For example, many non-verbal means of communication, such as American Sign Language, are clearly languages in their own right. On the other hand most instances where electro-magnetic and electro-mechanical impulses convey information, such as in radios and telephones, are cases where the signals in question are mapped from utterances or inscriptions by way of microphones and keyboards, then mapped back to utterances or inscriptions via speakers and printers or video-screens. Thus language appears to have a decided primacy as a means of communication.

The importance of language as a means of communication can be further brought out by noting that linguistic communication has a wider range of expression than does non-linguistic communication. This can be illustrated by contrasting a language, like English, with a graphical means of communication, like drawing pictures. Given the ability in English to make definitions and establish referential conventions, it seems clear that one can describe anything that one can draw (although often not nearly so perspicuously). On the other hand, one can discuss such things as evil, humor, gravity, air, time, and so on, even though one cannot draw them.

Given the centrality and importance of language as a means of communication, it seems most appropriate to base an investigation of information on linguistic communication, and the prime linguistic conveyors of information are sentences.

A second reason for basing this investigation on linguistic entities, like sentences, is that it is then possible to bring to bear the extensive findings about the way language works made available by linguistic and philosophical investigations of the last one hundred years.

The last reason for focusing exclusively on information carried by sentences is that intuitions about information seem clearer in this realm than in some others. For example, it seems much easier to say when two sentences carry the same information than it does to say when two pictures do. Since our analysis must perforce be based on intuitions about such questions (more about this later), it helps our cause to consider cases where these intuitions are the most solid.

1.1.3 The Convey/Contain Distinction

This investigation considers information carried by sentences. But sentences carry information in different ways. In everyday discourse, we frequently have occasion to distinguish between these ways by contrasting the information *contained* in a sentence or group of sentences with the information *conveyed* by a sentence or group of sentences. Thus, in investigating the way information is associated with sentences, one of the important things that must be looked into is the difference between containing and conveying information.

This seems straightforward enough, but it turns out that the matter is more complex than it appears on the surface. For (as we will see shortly) the convey/contain dichotomy is used in ordinary language to mark at least three important but very different distinctions. Thus, investigating the difference between a sentence's containing information and its conveying information requires that these three distinctions be sorted out, and that terminology be adopted to mark them unambiguously. The present section is devoted to this task.

The first distinction commonly marked by the convey/contain terminology involves the difference between the information carried by a sentence when it is taken literally and the information carried by the sentence in virtue of various subtle factors connected with its use, including its phrasing, the intonation employed by the speaker, the intentions of the speaker or writer, and so on. To illustrate this distinction, suppose that student X remarks to student Y "I'm really looking forward to that math test next week," but X's tone of voice and facial expression leave no doubt that in fact X is dreading the test. Then we might say that X's sentence *contains* the information that X is looking forward to the test, but X says the sentence in such a way that it *conveys* to Y the information that X is not looking forward to the test.

The distinction brought out in this example really depends on another distinction commonly made in philosophical and linguistic studies between what a person's *words* mean and what the *person* means when a sentence is used. The following passage from an article by Saul Kripke explains this distinction nicely:

> Let us distinguish . . . between what *the speaker's words meant*, on a given occasion, and what *he meant*, in saying these words, on that occasion. For example, one burglar says to another, "The cops are around the corner." What *the words meant* is clear: the police were around the corner. But *the speaker may well have meant*, "We can't wait around collecting any more loot; Let's split!" That is not *the meaning of the words*, even on that occasion, though that is *what he meant in saying those words, on that occasion* (Kripke 1977, 262).

Thus what a person's words mean may differ markedly from what the person means in using those words.

Given the distinction between what a person's words mean and what a person means in using certain words, we can unpack the distinction between the information contained and the information conveyed as follows: the information contained in a sentence S, on some occasion, is the information associated with S by virtue of what S means, on that occasion. In contrast, the information conveyed by S, on some occasion, is the information associated with S by virtue of what the utterer of S means in using S, on that occasion. Thus, returning to the example involving the students X and Y, X's sentence *contains* the information that X is looking forward to the test because X's *sentence means* that X is looking forward to the test. However, X's sentence *conveys* the information that X is not looking forward to the test because X *meant*, in uttering the sentence, that he or she was not really looking forward to the test.

When presented in this way, it is clear that this distinction between information contained and information conveyed has less to do with information than it does with certain details of the semantics and pragmatics of natural language. For the difference is only a by-product, so to speak, of the difference between what a person's words mean and what a person means in using certain words, on some occasion. The latter distinction, though it has important consequences for information science, is really quite beyond the boundaries of the field, falling instead in the domain of linguistics and the philosophy of language. As such, this distinction is outside the scope of this study and will not be investigated.

Nevertheless, this distinction will figure in subsequent discussion, particularly when the connection between information and meaning is considered (in section 4.1.2). At that time, the distinction will be referred to as a distinction between meanings, not as the distinction between information contained and information conveyed.

Furthermore, in order to avoid as many troublesome aspects of the theory of meaning as possible, attention is hereafter restricted (unless otherwise indicated) to what sentences mean, on given occasions, ignoring what people may mean in using them on those occasions.

In summary, the convey/contain terminology will not be used to pick out the distinction between what a person's words mean and what the person means in using certain words. This distinction will come up in later discussion of the connection between information and meaning, at which time the latter terminology will be used to mark it. Since the details and problems involved in drawing the distinction between what a person's words mean and what the person means are outside the scope of this study, they will not be addressed.

The second distinction typically marked by the convey/contain terminology has to do with the difference between sentences that could, but never are, used to pass a message and sentences that are actually used in this way. For example, suppose that the sentences I write in my diary are never read by anyone. Then we might say that the sentences in my diary *contain* information, since they express various statements about my life, my cat, the weather, and so on, but that they do not in fact *convey* any information to anyone, since no one ever reads them. These sentences *could* convey information, they just never do convey any.

It should be stressed that the sense of 'convey' used in this distinction is really quite weak. If someone reads and understands an information-containing sentence in my diary, then the sentence conveys information (in the present sense of 'convey'). It doesn't matter whether the reader believes that what the sentence says is true, whether the reader learns anything from the sentence, or in short whether the reader is affected in any way beyond coming to understand the sentence. (Of course, this ignores many substantive issues regarding the connection between information, truth, and belief. The reader is asked to put aside these issues until they are addressed in later chapters.) Information is conveyed to the reader if, so to speak, he or she "gets the message."

Another example will serve to further illustrate this distinction and also to substantiate the claim that the convey/contain terminology is used to mark this distinction in ordinary language. Consider the following passage:

> Melville survives shipwreck and is cast upon a desert island. Happening to find paper, pencil, and bottle, and knowing his latitude and longitude, Melville composes a few sentences containing information about his plight, deposits the paper in the

bottle, and throws it into the sea. With luck, the bottle will be found and opened, and the information conveyed to a responsible soul. With a bit more luck, the message will be believed to be genuine and a rescue mission dispatched to save poor Melville.

I suggest that this paragraph is perfectly good English, and that the words 'convey' and 'contain' are used in a typical fashion. Furthermore, these words are being used to mark the distinction under discussion.

This distinction will prove quite important in the course of our investigation. Thus I adopt the following terminology to mark it: the word 'contain' is used as it is above to refer to the information carried by a sentence independently of whether it is used to pass a message. So sentences contain information just by virtue of saying something about the world, that is, just by virtue of having truth conditions. But instead of 'convey', I use the word 'transfer' to refer to the information passed along by a sentence actually used to carry a message. Thus, for example, we say that my diary, and Melville's note, both *contain* information whether they are ever read or not; if someone reads and understands a sentence in my diary or in Melville's note, the sentence *transfers* information to him or her. A somewhat more precise characterization of this terminology will be given as soon as the third distinction is considered.

The third distinction often marked by the convey/contain terminology involves the difference between the information carried by a sentence apart from its being used to pass a message and what the receiver of a message learns from it—its "informative content," so to speak. Uses of the convey/contain terminology to capture this distinction are particularly common. For example, suppose I know neither the day nor the date, but I do know that the sixteenth is a Monday, the seventeenth a Tuesday, and so on. Then if I am told the date, I learn the day as well, so information about what day it is is conveyed to me by a message containing information about the date. The sentence 'Today is the seventeenth' conveys to me the information that today is Tuesday (as well as the information that it is the seventeenth), though the sentence only contains the information that today is the seventeenth.

The above example illustrates that more information may be conveyed by a sentence than is contained in it (in the present senses of 'convey' and 'contain'). Likewise, a sentence may contain more information than it actually conveys to a given individual on a given occasion. A good illustration of this point derives from the commonplace that in a deductively valid argument, "all the information or factual content in the conclusion [is] already contained, at least implicitly, in the premises" (Salmon 1973, 14). Yet the premises of a deductive argument don't generally convey (to most of us) the information expressed in the conclusion; otherwise we would not learn things from deductive arguments. To take a specific example, the information that the sum of the angles of a triangle in the plane is always two right angles is *contained* in Euclid's axioms and definitions. But this information is generally not *conveyed* to people who are presented with these axioms and definitions, no matter how well they understand them.

The sense of 'convey' under discussion also seems to be the one at work in statements like "He talked for hours, but he didn't convey much information." The point of such a statement may be that the speaker was not very informative—his listeners did not learn much from what he said. The speech, though, may have contained much information, in the sense that many substantive claims were made about the way the world is.

In all three examples of this use of the convey/contain dichotomy, the crucial feature pertaining to the use of 'convey' seems to be that the receiver of the message changes his or her beliefs as a consequence of the message. The "informativeness" of the message is the key feature. Furthermore, the information conveyed by a sentence is a function of this change in belief-state rather than a function of the information contained in the sentence.

Regarding the use of 'contain' in these examples, we see that this term is used to pick out the information associated with a sentence by virtue of its having truth conditions. In other words, 'contain' is used here as it is used above in discussing the contain/transfer dichotomy. Thus, in adopting terminology to mark the distinction now under discussion, we may retain both 'contain' and 'convey' without any danger of confusion with the contain/

transfer distinction. Hence I adopt the popular contain/convey terminology to mark the present distinction.

Of course, since the contain/transfer distinction and the contain/convey distinction have a term in common, it is somewhat misleading to view them as two two-way distinctions; there is really only a single three-way distinction: the contain/transfer/ convey distinction.

The contain/transfer/convey distinction figures prominently in the remainder of this study. Although more will be learned about this distinction in the course of our investigation, it behooves us to state as clearly as possible what is meant by these terms. Consequently, I formulate tentative analyses of these notions as follows:

> The *information contained* in a sentence S (if any) is the information carried by S in virtue of S's having truth conditions.

> The *information transferred* by a sentence S to some individual Y (if any) is that part of the information contained in S which is received and understood by Y.

> The *information conveyed* by a sentence S to an individual Y (if any) is the information associated with any change in Y's beliefs occasioned by Y's receiving and understanding sentence S.

These characterizations obviously leave much to be desired. However they will suffice for present purposes, and in any case will soon be amended as discoveries are made regarding these phenomena.

1.1.4 Information-How and Information-That

Another distinction that must be made in delimiting the scope of this study involves two senses of the term 'information'. The distinction between these two senses is very much like the distinction made in epistemology between 'knowing how' and 'knowing that' (see Lehrer 1974). Consequently, the latter distinction is considered first by way of introduction to the former.

If a person is said to know *how* to do something, then what is meant is that that person is competent, at least to a certain required minimal degree, to carry out a certain task. For example, if a person X knows how to drive a car, then X is at least minimally competent when it comes to driving cars. On the other hand, if someone is said to know *that* something is the case, then what is meant is that that person apprehends, under the appropriate circumstances, that a certain state of affairs obtains. If X knows that lemons are yellow, for instance, then we take it that X has been appraised of the color of lemons in some appropriate fashion and so is aware of this fact.

Turning to the case of 'information', we can make an analogous distinction between what we will call 'information-how' and 'information-that'. It is a commonplace to say that things like computer programs, algorithms, and recipes contain information. Now such information, in the case of the particulars just mentioned, is embodied in a sequence of instructions of one kind or another for accomplishing some task. For example, computer programs are instructions to machines about how to transform one class of computational states into another. A recipe is a sequence of instructions for preparing food. This instructional sort of information corresponds to "knowledge how" in epistemology, so we call information that consists of instructions about how to carry out a task or achieve a goal *information-how*.

Not all information is information-how, just as not all knowledge is know-how. There is also information to the effect that certain states of affairs obtain. Examples of this sort of information abound. Pretty much every indicative sentence can, under the appropriate circumstances, be said to carry information that something is the case. To consider a specific example, when Nixon resigned, headlines like "Nixon Resigns" carried the information that Nixon had resigned. Just as knowledge that a state of affairs obtains is 'knowledge-that', we define *information-that* as information to the effect that some state of affairs obtains.

A sequence of instructions is typically a sequence of sentences in the imperative mood, hence it is characteristic of information-how that it is carried by imperative sentences. In contrast, statements to the effect that some state of affairs obtains are usually expressed by sentences in the indicative mood, so it is characteristic of information-that that it is carried by indicative sentences. This pairing of information-how with imperative sentences and of information-that with indicative sentences is not ironclad, due mainly to the fact (discussed in section 1.1.3) that what a sentence means may differ from what a person means in using that sentence. However, if attention is restricted to what sentences mean irrespective of what the originators of sentences mean in using them, then this generalization does hold. Since we have chosen to pay attention only to what sentences mean, in this study, we will assume that information-that is carried by indicative sentences, and that information-how is carried by imperative sentences.

It is sometimes argued that knowledge how is always ultimately reducible to knowledge that. But whether this is so or not, it certainly is the case that the parallel reduction of information-how to information-that can be carried out. Information how to do some task T is a sequence of instructions t_1, t_2, . . . , t_n, all in the imperative mood. However, these instructions can be converted into an indicative statement in the following way: construct the sentence 'Task t can be accomplished by carrying out the following instructions: t_1, t_2, . . . , t_n'. This indicative sentence contains information-that. Any task that could be accomplished using the information-how of the sequence of instructions t_1, t_2, . . . , t_n, can still be carried out, so there seems to have been no loss in converting information-how to information-that. It follows that information-how is reducible to information-that.

It should be noted in passing that the converse reduction of information-that to information-how is not generally possible. The information that lemons are yellow, for example, staunchly resists attempts to express it as a sequence of instructions.

Our results about the reducibility of information-how and the irreducibility of information-that indicate that the latter sense of 'information' is primitive. Consequently our discussion will focus on 'information' in the sense of information-that. In addition, since information-that is associated with sentences in the indicative rather than the imperative mood, it may be more amenable to the eventual application of philosophical and linguistic methods. Finally, our intuitions again seem sharper with respect to information-that than with respect to information-how. For example it seems in general easier to decide when two indicative sentences carry the same information than it is to make such a decision involving two sequences of instructions. For all these reasons, we will hereafter deal virtually exclusively with information-that, and hence we will be particularly concerned with the information associated with indicative sentences. In terms of the stated goal of the study, this means that attention will be focused on the ordinary use of the term 'information,' in the sense of information-that, associated with indicative sentences.

1.1.5 Goals of an Analysis of Information

As stated, this study investigates the ordinary use of the word 'information' in the sense of information-that, particularly with respect to the ways it is contained in, transferred by, and conveyed by indicative sentences. In this section we summarize in greater detail the goals to be achieved by this investigation.

Perhaps the most valuable result of an examination of the notion of information would be an answer to the question "What, if anything, is information?" But it should be noted that there are really two questions embedded in this formulation, one depending on the answer to the other. The first question is, "Is there such a thing as information?" or "Does the word 'information' really designate anything?" If the answer to this first question is that information *is* some sort of thing, then there is the further question "What, exactly, is the thing that information is?" or "What does the term 'information' refer to?" If the answer to the first question is that there really isn't any such thing as information, then the second question obviously doesn't come into play.

We might call positions which give an affirmative answer to the first question *information realist* positions, and those which give a negative answer *information nominalist* positions. The conflict between these two sorts of positions has much in common with more traditional realist/nominalist debates, such as the controversies over the existence of mathematical objects like sets and numbers, and over the existence of abstract linguistic objects like meanings and propositions. One common element is that ordinary language seems to sanction realism. We talk as if there are sets, numbers, meanings, propositions, and information. (More technically, we quantify over such things. I am implicitly appealing to Quine's criterion of ontological commitment. See

Quine [1961, 12].) This means that the nominalist must explain away the apparent ontological commitment of our ordinary talk (or at least the "important" parts of it) to make nominalism tenable.

A second feature common to realist/nominalist debates in general is that the choice between the two alternatives must ultimately be made on the basis of their fruits. If a more powerful, simple, and fecund theory can be established given realism than can be established given nominalism, then realism wins. If a nominalist, however, can produce even as good a theory as the realist, then Occam's razor dictates that nominalism be preferred.

At present, there really are no well established theories of information of either a realist or a nominalist bent. Either position could be adopted in this study. However, the easiest course is to go along with ordinary language in subscribing to realism regarding information. For this reason, an information realist position is adopted here. Thus a fundamental premise of this work is that the first question above has an affirmative answer: there is an entity, or kind of entity, to which we refer when we use the term 'information'.

Granting that information is some sort of thing, one primary concern of this investigation is to determine as exactly and clearly as possible what this thing or sort of thing is. It should be understood that such an investigation requires some ontological spadework. For our puzzlement about the nature of information is so extensive that it comprehends even the most general properties and characteristics of information. This point can be made by considering a contrasting example. Were we investigating the nature of wood, for instance, we might aim to determine the chemical and structural features of this material, or perhaps its suitability as a building material, or its value as a fuel. One would not expect that the ontological features of wood would be considered, because the ontological characteristics of wood are not problematic. It is known, for example, that wood is the sort of thing that has spatio-temporal location. It is known that pieces of wood A and B are identical just in case A has the same spatio-temporal location as B. It is known that wood is not the sort of thing that has a truth-value, or that can be believed, and so on. Our understanding of information, however, is not nearly so extensive. It is not immediately clear whether information has spatio-temporal location, or whether it can have a truth value, or be believed. We are very much in the dark about the onto-logical character of information. Consequently one of our main tasks is to address the problem of the ontological character of information.

Such ontological investigation can profit by taking into account the findings of philosophers who have carried out similar in-vestigations of other sorts of things. It turns out that there are certain ontological sorts or categories that come up time and again in philosophical and conceptual analysis. These categories have been much discussed and explored, and in some ways are fairly well understood. Examples of such ontological categories or kinds include physical objects, sets, numbers, persons, prop-erties, universals, and so forth. If it can be shown that infor-mation does or does not fall into one or another of these categories, we will have gone a long way toward solving the problem of the ontological character of information. For then we will be able to claim that information does or does not have certain properties or characteristics of things of a particular ontological kind, and we will better understand the relationships between information and other types of things.

To sum up, in trying to provide an answer to the question "What is information?" and in critically appraising the answers to this question suggested by others, we will frequently have occasion to argue that information is or is not of a given onto-logical kind.

In addition to the ontological character of information, there are other important features of information that should be ex-plored. Recall the example of wood. Knowing about the onto-logical character of wood still leaves much to be specified in distinguishing wood from other things of the same ontological kind, like rocks, water, and peanut butter. Consequently, even if the question of the ontological character of information is set-tled, there are many other important features of information to be investigated.

One such important feature of information is that it is com-municated; one person may *inform* another. A large portion of this study will be devoted to examining the process of informing, both for its own sake, as a process intimately bound up with the phenomena of interest in information science, and for what the process of informing has to tell us about information itself.

Finally, we will be concerned throughout this book with two companion notions to information and informing: misinformation and misinforming. Although discussion will usually be carried on in terms of the former notions, conclusions will also be reached regarding the latter.

1.2 METHOD OF THIS STUDY

Analysis of the ordinary notion of information (and related concepts) is the goal of this study. As noted above, conceptual analysis is fundamentally a philosophical activity, so philosophical methods will be brought to bear in carrying out this task. The philosophical method employed in this study is that of contemporary analytic philosophy. Although a complete discussion and justification of this method is quite beyond the scope of this work, the following subsections summarize the method and offer some reasons to suppose that it is a legitimate means of philosophical investigation[†].

1.2.1 Semantic Ascent

Although the goal of this work is to investigate the nature of information (and related entities), much of the discussion up to this point has been about the *word* 'information' and how it is used, rather than about the *object* information. A glance through the rest of the book will show that this tendency characterizes the entire discussion. This shift from talk of objects to talk of words (which we follow Quine [1960, 271] in calling *semantic ascent*) is not accidental. In fact, it is the essential feature of the philosophical method adopted in this work. In this section, I briefly explain and justify the method of semantic ascent.

There are two main points to be made about semantic ascent. The first is that shifting from talk about objects to talk about

---

[†] Readers craving a more extensive treatment of this topic should consult the collections edited by Rorty (1967) and Lyas (1971), and the primer by Gorovitz, Hintikka, Provence, and Williams (1979).

words is *not* an abandonment of the effort to investigate objects—rather it is a way to investigate objects by means of examining words and how we use them. Second, semantic ascent is often a very useful thing to do; it produces (perhaps surprisingly) philosophical results. Quine makes both these points in his discussion of semantic ascent in *Word and Object*:

> Semantic ascent, as I speak of it, applies anywhere. 'There are Wombats in Tasmania' might be paraphrased as ' "Wombat" is true of some creature in Tasmania', if there were any point to it. But it does happen that semantic ascent is more useful in philosophical connections than in most, and I think I can explain why.
>
> Consider what it would be like to debate over the existence of miles without ascending to talk of 'mile'. "Of course there are miles. Whenever you have 1760 yards you have a mile." "But there are no yards either. Only bodies of various lengths." "Are the earth and the moon separated by bodies of various lengths?" The continuation is lost in a jumble of invective and question-begging. When on the other hand we ascend to 'mile' and ask which of its contexts are useful and for what purposes, we can get on; we are no longer caught in the toils of our opposed uses.
>
> The strategy of semantic ascent is that it carries the discussion into a domain where both parties are better agreed on the objects (viz., words) and on the main terms concerning them. Words, or their inscriptions, unlike points, miles, classes, and the rest, are tangible objects of the size so popular in the marketplace, where men [sic.] of unlike conceptual schemes communicate at their best. The strategy is one of ascending to a common part of two fundamentally disparate conceptual schemes, the better to discuss the disparate foundations. No wonder it helps in philosophy (Quine 1960, 271–272).

As Quine points out, if we can establish that 'Wombat' is true of creatures in Tasmania, then we know that there are Wombats in Tasmania. Finding something out about a word may amount to finding something out about an object. (And conversely, too, though this is less important for our purposes.) Hence we may indeed be able to find something out about information by focusing attention on 'information' and its uses.

The second point made in the passage above is that semantic ascent is often useful. Quine explains this in terms of carrying discussion into "a domain where both parties are better agreed on the objects (viz., words)" (Quine 1960, 272). In other words, it is easier to establish sound conclusions and to reach agreement regarding our use of language (and subsequently to extend these conclusions to defensible positions regarding the existence and nature of puzzling things like miles, sets, numbers, propositions, and information), than it is to establish defensible positions regarding these things directly.

I agree with Quine on this point. In support of this position I offer two arguments. The first is that the philosophical method based on semantic ascent has proven itself successful during this century, particularly in comparison to other methods employed over the course of the previous two thousand years. The second argument is aimed at reinforcing the claim that we can establish sound conclusions and reach agreement concerning our use of language by explaining how we can arrive at such conclusions. This argument is taken up in the next section.

In conclusion, in order to investigate the ordinary notion of information (and related concepts), we will employ the strategy of semantic ascent and focus our attention on the ordinary use of the term 'information' (and related terms). This approach will nonetheless yield conclusions regarding information, and these conclusions ought to be more secure and defensible than any arrived at by other means.

1.2.2 Language As a Rule-Governed Activity

One of the main points in favor of the strategy of semantic ascent is that it is fruitful, and one of the main reasons that it is fruitful is that it is possible to establish sound conclusions, and to reach agreement, concerning our use of language. Why is this so? The answer lies in the nature of language as a rule-governed activity whose rules can be ascertained by careful study.

A rule-governed activity is an activity with an associated set of rules such that one is doing the activity just in case one is acting according to the rules—and otherwise one is not doing the activity. Some of the best examples of rule-governed activities are games. Consider chess. The rules of this game specify that certain *movements* of the pieces on the board count as *moves* in the game. The activity of playing chess consists simply in making moves. If one moves a piece not in accordance with the rules, then one has not performed a chess move—one is not playing chess. In contrast, consider the activity of driving a car. There are no rules governing the activity of driving a car. There are natural laws that govern the movements of the car, but these are not rules because they cannot be broken. There are civil laws or regulations requiring that the activity be performed in a certain way, but these are not rules either. Failing to obey the speed limit is *not* failing to perform the activity of driving a car; if a car moves under someone's control then he or she is driving it, no matter whether well or badly, according to traffic laws or not.

It seems indisputable that language is a rule-governed activity. Certain ways of using words count as "moves" in the game, that is, as sentences of the language in question. Other "movements" are not part of the language because they don't follow the rules. To take a specific example, consider the inscriptions:

Does the book have a leather cover?

Book the leather does a have cover?

The first is an English question, the second is not. In fact the second simply is not English at all. The first inscription follows the syntactic rules of English, and so *is* English, the second does not, and is *not* English.

The further assertion that language is not only rule-governed but that we can uncover its rules is supported primarily by the past success of linguistic and philosophical investigations. Certainly the linguists' attempt, during the past thirty years, to make explicit the rules governing the syntax of various languages, particularly English, has been very successful. Similarly, the philosophical investigation of terms like 'truth,' 'knowledge,' 'evil,' and so forth, has been somewhat successful, though perhaps less so than that of the linguists.

Granting that using a language is a rule-governed activity and that we can discover its rules, then it is obvious how we can go about establishing firm conclusions about language: such conclusions amount to the discovery of the rules governing our use of language. Hence the success of the strategy of semantic ascent is grounded in the fact that we are able to discover the rules that govern our use of language.

1.2.3 Evidence About Use

We are interested in the rules governing the use of words. Note, however, that the *use* of a word is not the same as its *usage*. A use of a word, like the use of a knife, coin, or shovel, is a "way of operating" with something, or "a technique, knack, or method" (Ryle 1971, 48). In accordance with the fact that use is governed by rules, we can speak about misusing. On the other hand,

> a usage is a custom, practice, fashion or vogue. It can be local or widespread, obsolete or current, rural or urban, vulgar or academic. There cannot be misusage any more than there can be a miscustom or a misvogue (Ryle 1971, 48).

We are not interested in what people always, often, normally, or sometimes say. This is usage, and has to do with use only in that usage usually conforms to use. We are interested in what *can* be said in English rather than what is *typically* said. Consequently it will not do to examine a sample of speakers to determine what is said with respect to 'information'. This may tell us about the usage of the term, but not much about its use and the rules governing its use.

On the other hand, neither will it do to ask some sample of individuals what they mean by 'information'. Elaborate philosophical investigations of the use of language are only necessary because people in general are not very good at answering such questions, and particularly in the case at hand, they are not very good at figuring out what information is.

The way linguists and philosophers commonly attempt to determine the rules underlying use is to consider a wide variety of situations with the question "Is it legitimate to use the word here?" in mind. To quote John Austin, investigation proceeds "by examining *what we should say when*, and so why and what we should mean by it" (Austin 1971, 84). In this way, various rules of language can gradually be teased out and made explicit.

The method of considering what we should say when requires that decisions be made about whether words are being employed legitimately or not. Such decisions must be made by someone who has internalized the rules of a language, but anyone who does know the language will do. For, presumably, anyone who *really does* know a language will have internalized the same set of rules as other speakers. In particular, the present investigator is a native speaker and so presumably is competent to judge whether a given utterance or inscription is English. Therefore the arguments of this study rest on the linguistic intuitions of the present investigator, augmented by frequent discussions with others concerning their intuitions regarding various examples.

The linguistic intuitions that serve as the basis of many arguments in this book are not *necessarily* correct; not even a native speaker is infallible about his/her language. Readers must consult their own linguistic intuitions as well as evaluate the arguments of this study in determining whether to accept its conclusions about our language and about information. But to the extent that general agreement over intuitions and arguments is achieved, the results of this investigation may be regarded as reasonably well established conclusions about the rules governing our language, and hence ultimately about the concept of information embedded in our language.

1.2.4 Description Versus Prescription

So far, the job of providing a conceptual analysis has been characterized as a purely descriptive task: the aim is to discover and codify the rules that in fact govern our use of language. However, it is sometimes hard to tell whether a given analysis is purely descriptive or whether it moves into the realm of prescription—the realm of stipulating the use of language. The task of description is accomplished by advancing arguments based on various uses, or misuses, of certain terms, and so eventually eliciting agreement on the use of language, and reaching philosophical conclusions. However, as Maxwell and Feigl have pointed out, given an analysis, how are we to decide whether this is the correct description of [some use of language] or whether we should say that we have persuaded the ordinary man to accept "tightened up," perhaps modified—in short, *reformed*—meanings? Perhaps some cases are more aptly described in the former and others in the latter manner; but we know of no decision procedure for classifying each particular case, and we strongly suspect that many cases of putative ordinary-usage analysis are, in fact, disguised reformations (Maxwell and Feigl 1967, 193).

It seems that the task of providing descriptive analysis may often include some prescriptive analysis as well.

Furthermore, according to many philosophers, a purely descriptive analysis (if such can be achieved), may not be enough if we have certain goals in mind. Some tightening-up, or some resolution of ambiguity, may be needed to provide a good analysis in some cases. This point is suggested in a famous passage from John Austin's "A Plea for Excuses":

Certainly ordinary language has no claim to be the last word, if there is such a thing. It embodies, indeed, something better than the metaphysics of the Stone Age, namely . . . the inherited experience and acumen of many generations of men. But then, that acumen has been concentrated primarily upon the practical business of life. If a distinction works well for practical purposes in ordinary life (no mean feat, for even ordinary life is full of hard cases), then there is sure to be something in it, it will not mark nothing: yet this is likely enough to be not the best way of arranging things if our interests are more extensive or intellectual than the ordinary. And again, that experience has been derived only from the sources available to ordinary men throughout most of civilized history: it has not been fed by the resources of the microscope and its successors. And it must be added, too, that superstition and error and fantasy of all kinds do become incorporated in ordinary language and even sometimes stand up to the survival test . . . Certainly, then, ordinary language is *not* the last word: in principle it can everywhere be supplemented and improved upon and superseded. Only remember, it *is* the *first* word (Austin 1971, 86–87).

Ordinary language is the first word because it often embodies distinctions and various features of use that we must be careful of. But ordinary language is not sacrosanct because it is not always as simple, elegant, and philosophically respectable as we would like. Our language developed haphazardly over hundreds of years under the strain of the practical requirements of everyday use. Although this has made it into a complex and versatile tool of communication, it has also warped and misshapen it in certain ways. Hence it is often the case that once the ordinary use of a term has been established, certain infelicities crop up. A good explication of a term must straighten out these problems even though this may, and usually does, result in some divergence from ordinary use.

There is considerable tension between prescription and description in any attempt to provide a conceptual analysis, and the present attempt is no exception. Specifically in this case, the pull toward providing a purely descriptive account is provided by the goal of explicating the ordinary notion of information. A faithful description of this notion must be provided if I am to be justified in my claim to have analyzed *this* notion and not some other. On the other hand, the tendency to prescribe use is also present and may intrude without my even being aware of it. A further inducement toward prescription is provided by the fact that the ultimate goal of this work is to provide an analysis of information of use in information science, so a little prescriptive tightening-up of the notion of information may not be out of order.

In view of all this, I adopt the following policy with respect to description and prescription in this work. As Austin insists, ordinary language is the first word, but there has never been a sustained attempt to describe the ordinary language notion of information. Hence (in line with comments made earlier in this chapter) the best course at present is to take up the descriptive task. Even though the ordinary notion of information may best be altered in some ways to better suit it for information science, no recommendations on this score will be made in this study. Rather my goal will be to provide an accurate, adequate account of the notion currently underlying discussion in information science as a means of providing a firm basis for future decisions regarding such recommendations. However, in providing a clear and perspicuous analysis, it is still necessary to make a few stipulations, mainly to resolve ambiguities and other infelicities. For example, I have stipulated, and will continue to stipulate, conventions governing the use of the terms 'contain', 'transfer', and 'convey' with respect to the ways information is associated with sentences. This practice is forced by the need to resolve ambiguities in the ordinary use of 'contain' and 'convey', as discussed in section 1.1.3. But note that though I *prescribe* the use of these terms, my prescriptions are always intended to *describe* a certain ordinary use of 'contain' or 'convey'. Thus arguments based on use are still employed in justifying the stipulations I make regarding the notions of the information contained in, transferred by, and conveyed by sentences.

There is no way to rule out inadvertent prescriptive conclusions. However, note that a prescription regarding the use of a term must be at odds with the use of the term (otherwise it would be an accurate description). Hence prescriptions that claim to be descriptions can in principle always be ferreted out in the course of further inquiry. In other words, inadvertent prescription is just an instance of incorrect description, and though it is always possible to make a mistake, it is likewise always possible to catch mistakes and correct them.

1.2.5 Principles Governing Analysis

The activity of prescribing the use of a term should not be confused with that of making choices between alternatives in the course of descriptive analysis. Just as in physics the observations underdetermine theory, so that a choice must be made between alternative theories which are about equal in their ability to explain the facts, observation underdetermines theory in providing explications of terms, so choices must be made between alternative analyses. Also as in physics, there are principles governing such choices; in fact many of the principles governing analysis are identical to principles governing theory construction in physics and the other sciences.

The most important principle governing analysis is consistency. No analysis is adequate, or even intelligible, if it contradicts itself.

A second principle governing analysis is simplicity, particularly ontological simplicity. Simplicity is to be preferred in any theoretical account, and Occam's razor makes ontological simplicity particularly important in ontological investigations.

Finally, systematicity is an important feature to be considered when choosing between competing analyses. In general, explications that show systematic connections between related terms are to be preferred because of the value of global, coherent theories of ranges of phenomena.

In conclusion, it must be noted that although there are certain principles and requirements to which analysis must conform, the activities of providing an analysis, and of judging whether a suggested analysis is satisfactory, are as much arts as sciences and leave room for disagreement and controversy. Though perhaps unfortunate, this feature of conceptual analysis is apparently an ineluctable result of the difficulty of the task.

2
PRELIMINARY DISCUSSION OF INFORMATION

Before presenting my own analysis of information I will critically review discussions of information by information theorists and information scientists. This task of criticism is made much easier if certain aspects of the use of 'information' are settled beforehand so that there is some ground on which to base comments and criticisms. Consequently, this chapter carries out a preliminary investigation of 'information' as a preface to the next chapter.

The focus of discussion in this chapter is the ontological status of information. More precisely, I attempt to show that there are some things that information cannot be, although the question of what it indeed is is left for later.

Since information is closely bound up with the process of communication, I first consider the thesis that information is a process or event. Though this thesis is found to be untenable, the close connection between information and the process of communication is confirmed. Recalling that our concern in this essay is with information-that, and that information-that is typically communicated by indicative sentences, I next consider whether information might be sentences. In light of the type/token distinction, this investigation resolves into two parts: consideration of whether information might be sentence tokens, on the one hand, or sentence types, on the other. The conclusions are summarized in the last section of the chapter.

2.1 INFORMATION AS A PROCESS OR EVENT

There are many subtleties involved in determining what events and processes, and other related things like actions and procedures, are. Fortunately, we need only get so far in the investigation of such things as to establish that they (or their instances) are temporal entities, that is, they occur at a particular time or over some duration of time. For example, the event of my tripping over a curb begins and ends at particular instants; it has duration; there are times before it occurs, during which it is occurring, and after it occurs. A process, say the process of correcting a test paper, is likewise something that occurs (or has instances which occur) in time, and statements can likewise be made regarding the moments when it begins or ends, its duration, and so on.

A test of whether something is a process or event, then, is to consider whether it is (or has an instance which is) a temporal entity. If so, it will make sense to ascribe temporal properties, like duration, to the thing. It should also then make sense to say of the thing that there are times before, during, and after it occurs, and so on.

With this in mind, we turn to consideration of the following examples:

The information lasted two hours.

We'll meet right after the information.

She had to leave during the information.

The information begins at noon.

None of these sentences makes sense. Yet the sentences that result from these when 'information' is replaced by words that clearly refer to processes or events, like 'baptism', 'party', 'communication', 'correction of the test', and so forth, *do* make sense. The obvious conclusion is that information is not, and does not have instances which are, temporal entities. Thus information fails the test of whether something is an event or a process, so information is not an event or a process.

On the other hand, it seems clear that there are processes that involve information. When X calls Y on the phone and tells Y that P, for example, something begins, continues, and ends in time, and this temporal event involves information. Since information is not a process, there must be a distinction between information and the process of passing it from one place or person to another.

Likewise, we may consider the process or event that occurs when an individual Y changes his or her beliefs as a result of being given the information that P. A change in belief-state is something which occurs at a time or over some period of time, so it is a process or event. Since information is not a temporal entity, we must again distinguish between it and the process or event that occurs when someone changes his or her beliefs on the basis of receiving the information that P.

The processes or events described above clearly involve information, but they are distinct from information because the latter is a temporal entity. However, these processes involve *sentences*. Could it be that information is sentences? This question is taken up in the next section.

2.2 TOKENS AND TYPES

So far I have used the term 'sentence' without exactly specifying what I mean by it. That a more precise specification is called for is made evident if we consider these inscriptions:

The sky is blue.

The sky is blue.

How many sentences are there? Since there are two inscriptions, each of which can stand alone as a well formed English expression, one legitimate answer to this question is "two." On the other hand, both inscriptions are "really the same sentence," so the answer "one" is also defensible.

Such ambiguity in the use of 'sentence' is resolved by making the type/token distinction. The type/token distinction is a species of a more general distinction often made between universals and their instances. The latter distinction can be explained with an example. Although a lemon, a banana, and a dandelion are very different, they all have in common that they are yellow. One can say that these three things share the property or attribute of being yellow. This property or attribute of "yellowness" is called a *universal*, and the banana, lemon, and dandelion are said to *instantiate* the universal and to be *instances* of the universal. Lemons, bananas, and dandelions are spatio-temporal entities, and this is typical of instances of universals in general. The property of yellowness, however, is not located in space. Furthermore, it existed before there were any yellow things, will continue to exist once all yellow things have ceased to be, and would exist even if there had never been any yellow things at all. The property of yellowness is a timeless, abstract entity of some kind, as are all universals. (It should be noted that not all philosophers would agree with this characterization of universals; however, it is representative of positions employing universals.)

The type/token distinction is merely the universal/instance distinction made in the realm of symbolic expressions. Like the property of yellowness, an expression *type* is a timeless abstract entity of some sort which may or may not have instances. The instances of expression types are expression *tokens*. Hence expression tokens are spatio-temporal entities. The type/token distinction extends through the entire realm of symbolic expressions, so we distinguish word tokens from word types, sentence tokens from sentence types, paragraph tokens from paragraph types, and so on. It should also be noted that expression types may have verbal or written instances. The former are called *utterances*, and the latter *inscriptions*.

Returning to the consideration that prompted the introduction of the type/token distinction, we are now in a position to deal with the question posed above: "How many sentences are there?" In light of the type/token distinction, the clear and unambiguous answer to this question is that there are two sentence tokens, but they are instances of only one sentence type.

The thoughtful reader will no doubt have many questions regarding the details of type/token distinction, particularly with respect to the ontology of types and the exact relation between tokens and types. We needn't become mired in the niceties of the type/token distinction, however, since for our purposes only a few properties of types and tokens need be appealed to in the course of our discussion. As regards tokens, it should be clear that they are spatio-temporal entities and therefore have exactly the identity conditions that one would expect—tokens are identical just in case they have the same spatio-temporal co-ordinates. Since types are abstract entities, their identity conditions are more mysterious. At a minimum, we require of sentence types S and T that if they are identical, then the sequence of word types formed from any sentence token of sentence type S be the same as the sequence of word types formed from any sentence token of sentence type T. Or, stated less precisely but perhaps more intelligibly, sentence types at least have to have the same words in the same order to be identical. It turns out that no more precise specification of the identity conditions of types than this is required to carry out our discussion.

Armed with the type/token distinction, we are now in a better position to deal with the question "Is information a sentence or sentences?" by considering in turn whether information could be sentence tokens or sentence types.

To begin with sentence tokens, we know that tokens are spatio-temporal entities, and that consequently, tokens with different spatio-temporal locations are distinct. In particular, inscriptions A and B below are distinct tokens:

A.   Dandelions are yellow.

B.   Dandelions are yellow.

I take it that it is obvious, however, that the information carried by inscriptions A and B above is the same. From the point of view of information content, A and B are indistinguishable. Therefore information cannot be sentence tokens.

A second argument for the same conclusion is simply that we do not say that a sentence token *is* information, but that it contains or conveys information, that the token is merely the vehicle that carries some other thing. This strongly suggests that information indeed is something over and above inscriptions and utterances and confirms the conclusion that whatever information is, it isn't sentence tokens.

The alert reader will already have noted a similarity between our arguments against regarding information as a process or event on the one hand, and the latest argument against regarding information as sentence tokens, on the other. In both cases, we show that spatio-temporal properties come into play in important ways in the case of processes, events, and tokens, but not in the case of information; therefore information cannot be processes, events, or tokens. It is easy to see that virtually the same arguments can be redeployed to refute any claim that information is one or another kind of spatio-temporal object. For the identity conditions of spatio-temporal objects are always bound up with spatio-temporal location, which is not the case for information. Also, it always makes sense to ascribe spatio-temporal properties to spatio-temporal objects, while it does not make sense to do this in the case of information. Hence we conclude in general that information is not a spatio-temporal object of any kind. This conclusion will be a powerful tool in our discussion in the next chapters.

An objection arises regarding this conclusion, however. The objection is that it is simply false that we do not ascribe spatio-temporal properties to information, and that counter-examples to this claim abound. Consider the following:

You'll find the information on my desk.

She mailed the information last week.

Most of the information was destroyed in the fire.

The table is piled with information.

One can only find, mail, burn, and pile up spatio-temporal objects. Consequently information must be spatio-temporal after all.

The reply to this objection is based on a review of our use of the term 'number'. First, the point must be made that a *number* is an abstract mathematical entity of some sort. (This is, of course, a substantive philosophical thesis, but one which I trust is uncontroversial enough to be accepted by most readers.) Numbers do not have spatio-temporal properties, like location, and they certainly do not have such properties figuring in their identity conditions. *Numerals*, however, are another matter. Numerals are symbols, and there are numeral tokens and numeral types. Numeral tokens are spatio-temporal objects, so numeral tokens M and N are identical just in case they have the same location or spatio-temporal co-ordinates.

Now even though numbers are abstract entities, it is interesting to note that we commonly ascribe spatio-temporal properties to them in everyday talk. The following are examples pregnant for our discussion:

You'll find the numbers on my desk.

She mailed the numbers last week.

Most of those numbers were destroyed in the fire.

The table is piled with numbers.

We thus have a clear case in which a term designating an abstract entity is used as if it designates a spatio-temporal entity, and this occurs even though there is a common word designating the spatio-temporal entities in question, that is, 'numerals' (in the sense of numeral tokens). Our reply to the objection, then, is that it fails to establish a good case that use requires that information really be analyzed as a spatio-temporal entity. If 'number' can be used instead of 'numeral', then 'information' can be used instead of 'sentence token'. The objection fails, but our previous arguments still stand. Hence our conclusion remains that information is not a spatio-temporal object.

We might note in passing that the imprecision licensed by ordinary language with regard to 'number' and (in light of our conclusion) 'information', is an excellent example of a case where, in Austin's words, "ordinary language is *not* the last word" (Austin 1971, 87). For here we have a case where a very important distinction, from a philosophical point of view, is slurred over in ordinary use. The only thing to do in such cases is to take care in thinking of examples and following out consequences before drawing general conclusions.

We turn now to sentence types. Types are abstract entities, so it still may be that information is sentence types even though it cannot be sentence tokens. Much the same kind of arguments suffice to rule out this possibility, however. Consider the following sentences:

A.   It is raining.

B.   Water is falling from the clouds.

C.   Il pleut.

Above we noted that two sentence types S and T cannot be identical unless they at least are such that the sequence of word types formed from any sentence token of S is the same as the sequence of word types formed from any sentence token of T. On this criterion, the types of A, B, and C above are all distinct. Yet the information carried by all three is clearly the same. Hence information cannot be sentence types.

There is a further argument for this same conclusion. In everyday discourse about discourse, we occasionally make claims such as "That way of putting it may be more elegant than this, but it contains no more information." Ostensibly, the phrases "this way of putting it" and "that way of putting it" refer to sentence types rather than sentence tokens. For presumably what is at issue is not calligraphy or intonation but some feature of style having to do with the particular choice and order of words employed to say something. Now the sentence types referred to are not said to "be" the same information but to "contain" the same information. This suggests, as in the similar case of tokens, that information is something over and above sentence types, which uses the sentence types as a vehicle of conveyance. Hence our conclusion is once more that information is not sentence types.

2.3 CONCLUSION

I have shown that information is not a process or event, though it is bound up with communication processes. I have also shown that information is not inscriptions or utterances. By generalizing on the arguments used to establish these conclusions, I arrived at the position that information cannot be a spatio-temporal object at all. Although narrowing the possibilities significantly, this view still leaves open the entire realm of abstract entities as candidates for the ontological kind of information. This latter realm was narrowed somewhat by showing that information cannot be sentence types. We have therefore gotten so far as to be able to claim that information must be some kind of abstract entity, but not sentence types.

These conclusions provide the foundation for a critical review of the nature of information in the literature of information science, which is the topic of the next chapter. Investigation of the ontological character of information is therefore interrupted so that careful consideration may be given to competing accounts of the nature of information. The argument begun in this chapter is resumed in Chapter 4.

3
INFORMATION IN INFORMATION SCIENCE

In the first chapter I claimed that information science lacks an accepted characterization of the nature of information, and that the literature of the field is full of divergent proposals on this topic, none receiving the support of more than a handful of investigators. On this premise I argued that information scientists use the term 'information' substantially as it is used in everyday discourse, and that consequently an analysis of 'information' in its ordinary sense is required in, and in fact would substantially realize the goal of, providing an adequate analysis of the notion of information for information science. Implicit in that discussion was the claim that no explication of 'information' in the information science literature at present *is* adequate as an analysis of the term in its ordinary sense. In this chapter I review the information science literature in order to show that there indeed is wide disagreement concerning the nature of information among information scientists, and that none of the explications in the literature is adequate as an analysis of 'information' in its ordinary sense.

3.1 SURVEYS OF THE LITERATURE

One means of establishing the diversity of opinion regarding the nature of information among information scientists is to review the literature; another way is to make use of the work of others and point out that this fact has already been well established by past reviewers. Survey discussions of attempts to define 'information' are quite common in the information science literature and range from short discussions of only a few works (like the articles by Artandi [1973], Belkin [1975], and Rathswohl [1975]), to extensive reviews [like those of Belkin [1978], Wellisch [1972], and Wersig and Neveling [1975]). In this section I summarize some of the findings of the latter three reviews.

The first of these three to be published was Hans Wellisch's 1972 article "From Information Science to Informatics: A Terminological Investigation." In this essay Wellisch's main concern is to review the literature to find out what information science is, and whether it is really a science. He found thirty-nine definitions of 'information science' published between 1959 and 1971, but they unfortunately were completely at odds with one another—the definitions hardly even had any *words* in common with one another. Says Wellisch,

> the picture that emerges is one of utter diversity and lack of agreement on even a single basic concept underlying the discipline of [information science], except, of course, the concept of "information" itself which, however, is also highly ambiguous and mostly ill-defined (Wellisch 1972, 165).

More specifically with respect to the concept of information, Wellisch found that only eight individuals bothered to try to define 'information'. Wellisch goes on to note that

> even the eight valiant definers of "information" as the central concept with which [information science] is concerned do not succeed to arrive [sic.] at an agreed-upon definition, nor do their definitions have any common elements (Wellisch 1972, 171).

Wellisch substantiates this claim by reviewing the eight definitions and showing that they indeed do not have anything in common. He also incidentally succeeds in demonstrating that several of them are quite unworkable.

In summary, then, Wellisch's article presents good evidence of the lack of agreement about what information is among information scientists.

In 1975, Wersig and Neveling published "The Phenomena of Interest to Information Science." Like Wellisch, Wersig and Neveling are most interested in determining what information science is, but, like Wellisch again, they resort to a review of definitions of 'information' because of the truism that "information science investigates information." In the section of their article in which such definitions are considered, Wersig and Neveling begin as follows:

> The most extreme case of polysemy in the technical communication of information and documentation is the term 'information'. A semantic analysis made by one of the authors showed that there are at least six different approaches to the use and understanding of the term in the whole field of disciplines (Wersig and Neveling 1975, 129).

The "semantic analysis" mentioned in this quotation is the basis for the subsequent discussion of various definitions. It must be understood that by "six different approaches," the authors do *not* mean six different definitions; they mean many definitions (seventeen, in fact) that they managed to group into six broad categories for the purposes of discussion. Even within categories, however, the definitions are typically very different from one another. To take an example, one of the broad categories or approaches distinguished by Wersig and Neveling is the "process approach," according to which information is defined as some sort of process or event. The two definitions subsumed under this category are:

> Information . . . is a process which occurs within a human mind when a problem and data useful for its solution are brought into productive union.

> Information . . . is a set of purpose-directed actions covering the following elements: generation . . . , transmission, storage, and inquiry (Wersig and Neveling 1975, 132).

Thus on the one hand information is defined as a certain mental process and on the other as something (it is not really clear what) that at least is not a mental process. Similar diversity occurs among the definitions in the other five categories.

Wersig and Neveling go on to propose their own characterization of information science, and from it they derive yet another definition of information, different from all those they survey (their definition is considered in section 3.4 below). This makes a grand total of eighteen quite distinct definitions of 'information' exhibited in the Wersig and Neveling article. The point, once again, is that information science is completely lacking in an accepted view concerning the nature of information.

By far the most complete and informative review of proposed definitions of 'information' that has yet appeared is Belkin's 1978 survey "Information Concepts for Information Science." Belkin reviews a representative portion of the literature on this topic instead of attempting an exhaustive investigation. His rationale is that:

> The literature of information science is littered with "one-line" information definitions which can normally be classified into one of a small number of types of information concepts, each of which usually has some well-developed exemplar. . . . In order fairly to judge the value of any information concept, one needs access to the reasoning behind the proposal and some indications of its possible consequences. Therefore, this review becomes a critical survey of approaches to an information concept for information science, with one or more examples of each approach discussed in some detail, rather than an exhaustive survey of the literature (Belkin 1978, 55–56).

Though there may be some question whether the myriad one-line information definitions can really be plausibly classified into categories characterized by having a well developed exemplar, Belkin includes enough exemplars and approaches to achieve a survey representative of the wide diversity of views in the field. Specifically, he distinguishes eleven "approaches to an information concept" and presents and examines sixteen definitions of 'information'. Furthermore, none of the important discussions have been left out (as frequently happens in other surveys of definitions of 'information').

Besides being a useful compendium of definitions of 'information', Belkin's article stands out as being one of the few in which various proposed definitions are subjected to thorough criticism. Although there is considerable question whether Belkin's criteria of adequacy for an information concept are acceptable or appropriate, many of his criticisms are nevertheless enlightening and very much to the point.

Despite the suggestion implicit in Belkin's reference to various "schools of thought" that there are only a few competing approaches to the question of the nature of information, his identification of nearly a dozen such "schools" indicates that there is not really that much agreement on this question in the field. Belkin's article therefore adds to the evidence from the surveys by Wellisch, and Wersig and Neveling that information science lacks an accepted characterization of the nature of information, and that the literature of the field is full of divergent proposals on this topic, none receiving support from more than a few investigators.

3.2 INFORMATION AS A SPATIO-TEMPORAL ENTITY

It is frequently proposed in the information science literature that information is some sort of spatio-temporal entity. Several such proposals are reviewed in this section. The kinds of things most often suggested in this regard are tokens and processes or events. Explications which take the former approach are treated in subsection 3.2.1, those that take the latter in subsection 3.2.2.

In Chapter 2, it was shown that information cannot be a spatio-temporal entity, and that in particular it cannot be either tokens or some kind of process or event. We therefore already know that the definitions reviewed in this section are inadequate on ontological grounds. Consequently we need not bother to rehearse this objection in the course of scrutinizing each suggested definition.

3.2.1 Information as Tokens

The view we examine in this subsection is expressed by Farradane in two recent articles (1976 and 1979). Farradane begins by noting the concerns of information scientists:

> There is no doubt that we are concerned with human intercommunication which, omitting the possibility of direct thought transference, always involves some medium of communication (Farradane 1976, 96).

Thoughts must be converted into a medium of communication and back again, so these processes are of interest. However, "the manipulation of the various forms of the representation of thought is the main consideration in communication" (Farradane 1976, 99), so the primary thing of interest in information science is the medium of communication. Farradane tells us that the most common medium is language, along with "other communication media which one can call language" (Farradane 1976, 18), including graphical means of representation, music, and the symbols of mathematics.

On this basis, Farradane suggests that information is

> any physical form or [sic.] representation, or surrogate, of knowledge, or of a particular thought, used for communication (Farradane 1976, 13).

Farradane does not explain himself any further, nor does he defend this characterization of information. Although he does not use the term, it seems plausible, given the above quotation and the context in which it occurs, to understand Farradane to mean that information is (or includes) tokens, and specifically tokens used in communication to express or transfer someone's knowledge or beliefs. This seems plausible because, to begin with, the quotation and its context suggest that Farradane is referring to entities that are part of a symbolic system of communication, like language, hence to symbol types or tokens. His use of the term 'physical' further suggests that it is tokens to which he is referring. Finally, the quotation is quite clear in specifying that the "representation, or surrogate," that is, token, must be used in communication to transfer knowledge or belief.

As mentioned above, the position that information is tokens was refuted in Chapter 2. Even if this position were acceptable, however, Farradane's requirement that tokens be used for the communications of someone's thoughts, beliefs, or knowledge before they can be considered information does not square with our ordinary use of 'information', particularly in the idiom of the information "contained" in a sentence or group of sentences. This can be established by considering the following example.

Suppose a robot spacecraft is sent to a distant planet and carries out various experiments and measurements. Suppose the spacecraft determines that, say, the atmosphere of the planet is fifty percent nitrogen, and that it prepares to send the message "The atmosphere is fifty percent nitrogen" by producing a token of this message for input to its transmitter. Finally, suppose that just as it is about to send the message, an alien tree falls on the spacecraft and destroys its transmitter. The message is never sent, and due to cutbacks in the budget of the space program, no other spacecraft is ever sent to that planet. The token produced by the spacecraft to the effect that the planet's atmosphere is fifty percent nitrogen expresses no one's thoughts, beliefs, or knowledge, nor is it ever used for communication. Hence on Farradane's account, the spacecraft does not have the information that the atmosphere of the planet is half nitrogen. Yet surely the spacecraft *does* have this information, at least according to what is ordinarily meant by the word 'information.' Consequently Farradane's view, even aside from its ontological deficiency, fails as a characterization of information by placing unjustifiable restrictions on what counts as information.

Our conclusions regarding Farradane's view, then, are that it fails on ontological grounds as a characterization of information, and that even if it were ontologically acceptable, it still fails to reflect our ordinary use of the term 'information'.

3.2.2 Information as a Process or Event

In this subsection we review two versions of the general position that information is a process or event. Specifically, we consider Debons' view (Debons 1978) that information is a process, and Pratt's view (Pratt 1967, 1977) that it is an event.

Debons' ideas regarding the nature of information are often alluded to (Otten 1974; Dow 1977) but not often explicitly or clearly stated. The most straightforward presentation of Debons' position appears in a 1978 paper called *Determining Information Function*, but, as we will see, his view is none too clearly ex-

pressed even there. His position is based on a distinction between two "senses" of information: information as a commodity
and information as a process. Although we are mainly concerned
with the latter sense, it might be noted in passing that the former
sense is of information as tokens. For, regarding information as
a commodity, Debons states that,

> in this sense, information is the physical representation of events
> and states in the environment, structured so as to be intelligible
> to a user or group of users (Debons 1978, 2).

We see that this characterization of information is but an instance
of the species that analyzes information in terms of tokens, and
is thus subject to the objections developed in Chapter 2. Consequently we need not bother with a detailed criticism of Debons'
notion of information as a commodity.

Debons' characterization of information as a process begins
as follows:

> Information is a process whereby data are received and interpreted
> by an intelligent being, which transforms the data in light of its
> existing view of the world, thus leading to a change in state of
> the receiver, who is then "informed" (Debons 1978, 2).

The process described by Debons in this passage is apparently
a "mental" process carried out by an individual interacting with
the world. As such this process of information apparently does
not include "external" processes such as those carried out by
information systems which gather and process data for dissemination to users. With this in mind, consider the following passage, which occurs a few sentences after the one given above:

> Information, then, is viewed as a process through which data
> from the environment are captured, and processed to facilitate
> interpretation by a user (the commodity of information); and then
> transformed by a user in such a way as to change his state of
> knowledge about the environment (the process of information)
> (Debons 1978, 2).

This passage suggests that the process of information encom-
passes the entire procedure of gathering, arranging, and dis-

seminating data to users (presumably carried out by an information system), as well as the business carried out by a user in understanding and interpreting data once it is received. Furthermore, the parenthetical reference to the process of information at the end of this passage is apparently meant to suggest that the transformation of data "by a user in such a way as to change his state of knowledge about the environment" *is* the process of information. In other words, Debons explains the process of information as a process that includes as a proper part the process of information. But this is unintelligible. Nor does this problem arise from a mere infelicity of wording in the second passage. Debons supplies a diagram of the entire process of collecting, storing, arranging, retrieving, and disseminating data to a user, who then interprets and incorporates the data. This figure is labeled "INFORMATION (as a process)."

Debons is obviously very confused about what he means by the phrase 'the process of information'. Even if this confusion were to be cleared up, however, there is still the difficulty, discussed in Chapter 2, that our ordinary use of the term 'information' precludes an analysis in terms of processes or events. Therefore, even though at this point there is considerable question about exactly what Debons' position on information as a process is, this position is undoubtedly unacceptable on ontological grounds.

The second example of the view that information is a process or event is much more clearly worked out than the first. Alan Pratt's position is set forth in two publications, appearing in 1967 and 1977. The latter discussion, besides being more recent, is also more extensive than the former, so my review focuses on it. Pratt's position regarding the nature of information is based on a model of the communication process also set forth in the 1977 article. This model in turn is based on a model of human understanding and cognition promulgated by Kenneth Boulding in his book *The Image* (1956). The central notion in all this is that of an "Image."

An Image is a person's world-view, including beliefs about matters of fact, values, customary ways of looking at and thinking about things, and so forth. Everyone's Image is different from everyone else's because no two people have had exactly the same experiences. A person's Image is the main factor determining how he or she reacts to experience. Thus different people react in different ways to experience. Communication is the process of individuals acting on one another to alter each others' Images. In order for communication to be successful, there must be a certain similarity or congruence between the Images of the people involved—otherwise they will not understand or believe each other. For example, successful communication requires that the recipient of a message have a "predisposition" corresponding to the sender's "purpose." "Predisposition includes the recipient's ability, and his willingness, to have his Image altered in the manner intended by the source" (Pratt 1977, 211). By exploring such constraints on the process of communication, Pratt establishes his own model of human communication as a model of the factors involved in the process of one person's succeeding in altering the Image of another.

Once Pratt has constructed his model, he considers its consequences regarding the nature of information. If the conditions of the model are met, and one person succeeds in sending a message to another who understands it and alters his/her Image accordingly, then

> in ordinary speech we say that he has become *informed* about the matter at hand. This is a surprisingly precise and accurate statement. He has been "in-formed" (L. in = in, within; formere = shape or form). He has been altered or affected.
> In-formation is the alteration of the Image which occurs when it receives a message. Information is thus an event; an event which occurs at some unique point in time and space, to some particular individual. More precisely, "information" is the name of a class of events, like the word "explosion" (Pratt 1977, 215).

The words 'inform' and 'information' are thus closely related in that they both have to do with the event that occurs when someone's Image is altered in light of a message. The verb 'inform' refers to the activity of changing an Image through communication, and 'information' is the noun that refers to the event. Informing is the activity of causing information to occur.

The first point to note in assessing the adequacy of this explication is that one ought not get too carried away with the

Latin underpinnings of 'inform'. This word does come from the Latin *informere*, as Pratt notes. However, according to the *Oxford English Dictionary* (1933), the use of 'inform' to mean "to form or shape" is obsolete. Thus, although Pratt's use of the term to mean "changing a person's Image" is felicitously coincident with its obsolete use as a Latin derivative, it does not reflect contemporary use. Pratt has extended the ordinary use of 'inform' to carry some of the consequences of his model.

This extension is not too troublesome in itself; however, it has the unfortunate result of encouraging a cognate use of the term 'information'. Pratt makes the jump from using 'inform' to designate the activity of using a message to alter someone's Image to using 'information' to designate the event; this is the thrust of the passage quoted above. It is also Pratt's only reason for claiming that information is an event.

Although Pratt's view regarding the nature of information flows naturally from his model of the communication process, and provides a pleasing coherence between the uses of 'inform' and 'information', it unfortunately runs afoul of our ordinary use of the term 'information'. Pratt refutes himself on these grounds, in fact, when he goes on to expand his comparison between the words 'information' and 'explosion'. He points out that:

> explosions cannot be stored or retrieved. One may, of course, store and retrieve potentially explosive substances, or potential explosions, just as one may store and retrieve potentially informative substances—artifacts which, under the appropriate conditions, may cause an "information" to occur. ("Informative event" is perhaps a more felicitous term.) (Pratt 1977, 215).

In this passage, Pratt generates a counter-example to his analysis. It is the clause "may cause an 'information' to occur." This clause does not make sense. Pratt implicitly admits this by putting 'information' in scare-quotes and suggesting that the phrase 'informative event' may be more "felicitous." It is almost as if Pratt is admitting that he isn't really talking about what we ordinarily mean by 'information', but rather about an informative event. But then Pratt's explication is not an analysis of 'information' but of 'informative event'.

A further difficulty with Pratt's position is his claim that the event which information is supposed to be is an alteration of someone's Image. Such an event is necessarily "within a person"; perhaps it is some sort of mental event. In any case, on Pratt's account there is no information if effective communication fails to take place. This result, however, leaves one at a loss to explain certain common uses of 'information' in cases where no communication occurs. For example, if no one ever sees these pages, and they never serve to effect any change in anyone's Image, then on Pratt's analysis (it seems) they contain no information. But surely this is incorrect. These pages contain information about what Pratt and others have claimed regarding the nature of information, for instance, and other information besides.

In light of all these objections, plus the general objection, on ontological grounds, against explicating 'information' in terms of processes or events, we conclude that Pratt's view concerning the nature of information is unacceptable.

3.3 INFORMATION THEORY

The task of this chapter is to review discussions of the nature of information in the core literature of information science. Information theory (also called "the mathematical theory of communication") is a field distinct from information science, so it may seem inappropriate to devote a section of this chapter to the information theoretic approach to the notion of information. There are, however, important historical reasons for including a discussion of the information theoretic approach to information in this chapter.

Information science began to establish itself as a distinct discipline in the mid to late fifties and the early sixties. During this period there was a great deal of excitement over the promise of information theory, which itself had only become firmly established as a soundly based engineering discipline with the publication, in 1948, of Claude Shannon's seminal work "The Mathematical Theory of Communication." The excitement was not so much over the importance of Shannon's work for the engineering of telephone, telegraph, and computer systems (which was its main point), but over the possible application of

Shannon's model of communication and his mathematical formulations to myriad problems in human communication, ranging from the physiology of perception to the semantics of natural language.

An excellent example of this sort of attitude is an article by Anatole Rapoport which appeared in 1953. In this article, Rapoport summarizes Shannon's work and then suggests that

> It may be true that the technical problems of long range communication (radio, television, etc.) can be treated entirely independently of the semantic content of the messages or the semantic reactions of the audience. But it may also be true that the methods involved in treating these problems (for example, the mathematical theory of information) can be applied in the seemingly different contexts of the events which interest general semanticists, psychologists, and others (Rapoport 1970, 9).

Although Rapoport goes no further than this in suggesting exactly how Shannon's work "can be applied in the seemingly different contexts" that he mentions, his optimism in this regard is quite typical of the times.

Given this sort of optimism about Shannon's work, it is not surprising that the nascent field of information science was caught up in the rush to exploit Shannon's discoveries. As a result, the information theoretic approach to information was a standard paradigm in information science in its early years.

As the fifties drew to a close, however, it became increasingly obvious that Shannon's work could not profitably be applied wholesale to realms outside information theory (although even now some information scientists persist in believing that information theory can somehow be altered or extended in some way to provide the theoretical underpinnings of the field; see Artandi [1973], Brookes [1975], or Fairthorne [1975], for example). The predominant current attitude among information scientists regarding the significance of information theory for information science is well expressed in the following passage from Whittemore and Yovits:

> ['Information'] is frequently used rather specifically in the sense that Shannon and Weaver have established in their treatment of

"information theory," more accurately called "communication theory" . . . While this may indeed be of interest in information science, it is certainly not the major nor even a large part of information science. Such a treatment does not consider the really important areas of concern, almost all of which are involved with the context, meaning, and effectiveness of messages . . . the Shannon and Weaver approach is generally agreed to be too restrictive to be of wide interest with regard to the formulation of an information science (Whittemore and Yovits 1973, 222).

Thus, although the relevance of information theory for information science is rather a dead issue, the historical importance of information theory in the development of information science calls for the inclusion of a discussion of information theory in this review.

Nevertheless, my discussion of information theory will be quite abbreviated, mainly because the theory is technically complex but readily shown to be irrelevant to our concerns in this work. A detailed examination of information theory would simply not generate a return sufficient to justify the investment of time and space required.[†] Consequently, the next few subsections will only summarize the information theoretic approach, along with some of its derivatives. The final subsection shows why these accounts fail as analyses of the ordinary notion of information.

3.3.1 Summary of Information Theory

Information theory is wholly concerned with the problem of faithfully transmitting a message from one place to another. The theory is mathematical in character, but finds wide application in computer science and telecommunications. Some of its main topics are the efficient coding of messages, error detection and correction in transmitted messages, and the capacity and reliability of transmission channels. Information theory is thus primarily an engineering discipline concerned with a narrow range of problems. In particular (and this will be important later on),

---

[†] Detailed presentations of information theory abound. Jones (1979) is a good introductory text. The best philosophical considerations of information theory are the articles by Bar-Hillel in *Language and Information* (1964), and Dretske's recent book *Knowledge and the Flow of Information* (1981).

the scope of information theory is restricted to the transmission of messages *distinct from any interpretation*. This has been an explicit feature of information theory at least since Shannon made the point in 1948:

> The fundamental problem of communication is that of reproducing at one point either exactly or approximately a message selected at another point. Frequently the messages have *meaning*; that is they refer to or are correlated according to some system with certain physical or conceptual entities. These semantic aspects are irrelevant to the engineering problem (Shannon 1948, 3).

Messages need not have any interpretation at all. For the purposes of analysis in information theory it suffices that a set of messages be specified, and that any message actually sent or received be chosen from this set.

Information theory distinguishes and separately deals with *discrete*, *continuous*, and *mixed* communication systems. In discrete systems, messages are sequences of discrete symbols, an example being telegraphy. In a continuous system, messages are continuous functions; examples of continuous systems are radio and television. Finally, mixed systems are those in which both discrete and continuous messages occur. Our discussion need only cover discrete systems.

Mathematical models of discrete systems are framed in terms of finite sets of messages that may be transmitted or received. Let $M = \{m_1, m_2, m_3, \ldots, m_n\}$ be such a set of messages. Associated with the members of M are various probabilities; associated with message m_i is the probability p_i that m_i will be transmitted, the probability q_i that it will be received, and the conditional probability p_{ij} that m_i was transmitted given that m_j is received.

Information theory defines various quantities on the basis of these probabilities. Each message has a value called its 'self-information', 'surprisal', 'selective information', or simply 'information'. This quantity is defined as follows:

> The *self-information*, $I(m_i)$, of a message m_i at a source (or destination) is $-\log(p_i)$ (or $-\log(q_i)$).

(The choice of base for the logarithm is irrelevant as long as it is used consistently. However, base 2 is universally employed by information theorists.)

The self-information of a message is supposed to be a measure of the information associated with the message. It is mainly employed by information theorists as a stepping-stone in the course of calculating the quantity they are really interested in, namely the entropy, or average information, associated with a source (or destination):

> The *entropy*, H(M), of a set of messages M at a source (or destination) is the expected value of the self-information of the messages, i.e.,
>
> $$H(M) = \Sigma p_i I(m_i) = \Sigma(-p_i)\log(p_i)$$
>
> (or the same with q_i substituted for p_i, if calculations are made with respect to the destination).

The entropy is supposed to be a measure of the uncertainty regarding which message will be chosen from M.

The notions of self-information and entropy are extended in a straightforward manner (using conditional probabilities) to measures of *conditional self-information* and *conditional entropy*, which are supposed to be measures of information and uncertainty, respectively, except that they are associated with whether a given message was transmitted over the communication channel given that another message is received. These latter notions, particularly conditional entropy, provide much of the power and utility of information theory for engineering applications. The conditional probabilities of the messages in M depend on the reliability of the channel over which transmission takes place, so the conditional entropy (and a few other related quantities) provide measures of the noise on a channel, the fidelity of transmission, and the trustworthiness of received messages.

It should be stressed that the key notion in information theory is entropy rather than self-information. This makes perfect sense when one realizes that the main concern of the theory is the general study of communication systems rather than the communication of particular messages—one expects such a theory to study the "average" behavior of the system rather than its behavior in particular cases.

This completes our summary of information theory. Though brief, this summary has exhibited the main assumptions and aims of the theory and demonstrated its tone and emphasis, which are the points of interest for the discussion below of the adequacy of this theory's approach to information.

3.3.2 Inadequacy of the Information Theoretic Approach

My comments concerning the relevance of the information theoretic approach for the task of providing an adequate analysis of the ordinary notion of information focus on two points. First, I argue that information theory has very little to contribute to this task because it is neutral regarding most of the questions that this investigation seeks to answer. Second, I suggest (following Bar-Hillel [1964]) that even regarding the portion of the analytic task concerning which information theory apparently has something to contribute (namely the measurement of the amount of information associated with a message), it is *not* information theory which is relevant, but another theory, resembling information theory in the calculus that it employs, that is really of interest.

In the first chapter, it was suggested that an adequate analysis of the ordinary notion of information should (ideally) attempt to say what sort of thing information is, what misinformation is, and what is involved in the processes of informing and misinforming. These questions involve inquiries into the relationships between information and truth, belief, and knowledge, as well as consideration of the ontological status of information. Information theory addresses *none* of these topics. The entire theory is formulated mathematically in terms of the probabilities that certain sequences of symbols will be transmitted or received over a communication channel. Questions involving truth, belief, and knowledge never enter the picture. Even a proponent of the position that information theory is relevant to the philosophical analysis of information (namely Fred Dretske), admits that

communication theory does not tell us what information is. It ignores questions having to do with the *content* of signals, what *specific information* they carry, in order to describe *how much* information they carry (Dretske 1981, 41).

Dretske could have added that communication theory also ignores questions having to do with the beliefs, intentions, reliability, and other features of the informant and informee in processes of informing.

In neglecting so many crucial issues, information theory forfeits any chance of being a legitimate candidate for providing an adequate analysis of the ordinary notion of information. (Of course, this was never the goal of information theory anyway.)

Though unable to provide an analysis on its own, information theory may still provide the definitive treatment of the notion of the *amount of information* associated with a message. As noted above, however, I follow Bar-Hillel (1964) in arguing that information theory fails even here to contribute to the task of analyzing the ordinary notion of information.

To begin with, it is clear that the ordinary notion of information involves a component that enables us to make comparisons of the "amount" of information associated with a sentence. As Bar-Hillel notes,

> it is quite customary to compare statements, in ordinary language, with respect to the information that they convey. It makes full sense to say, for instance, that a report "The enemy attacked at dawn" conveys less information than "The enemy attacked in battalion strength at 5:30 A.M." . . . It is therefore sensible to ask whether one could not refine the comparative evaluation into a quantitative one and tell *how much more information* is conveyed by the second report over that conveyed by the first one (Bar-Hillel 1964, 286).

We can certainly agree that a quantitative account that accords well with our pre-analytic qualitative evaluations would be a desirable refinement, as Bar-Hillel says.

Does information theory provide such a refinement? Bar-Hillel suggests not, the problem being the distinction between the statement made by a given sequence of symbols (which seems to be the crucial item involved in the comparative evaluation) and the sequence of symbols itself (which, of course, is the sole basis for the quantitative evaluation provided by information theory). In Bar-Hillel's words, the problem is that

> *there is no logical connection whatsoever between . . . the amount of (semantic) information conveyed by a statement and the measure of the rarity of kinds of symbol sequences* [i.e., the self-information of a message]. The event of transmission of a certain statement and the event expressed by this statement are, in general, entirely different events (Bar-Hillel 1964, 286).

We may illustrate this objection using the example in the passage first quoted from Bar-Hillel above. Suppose that Jones is a very precise and responsible officer, so that when Jones reports to his superior Smith concerning the enemy's activities, it is more likely that Jones will say "The enemy attacked in battalion strength at 5:30 A.M." than that Jones will say "The enemy attacked at dawn." Then according to information theory, there is more information associated with the latter sentence than with the former. But this fails to accord with our pre-analytic intuitions. Hence information theory cannot be considered to provide an adequate theory of our ordinary notion of the amount of information associated with a message. The problem, as Bar-Hillel points out so clearly, is that the likelihood that a particular string of symbols is used to pass a message has nothing to do with the quantity of information (in the ordinary sense) associated with the message.

In reply to this criticism, it may be suggested that the probabilities associated with messages be the probabilities of occurrence of the events designated by the messages rather than the probabilities that the messages will be transmitted or received. Typically, however, this will not work because it results in certain mathematical requirements of the theory being violated. However, another theory has been developed that makes use of probabilities associated with events as a means of quantifying the amount of information associated with a sentence. This theory, called the *theory of semantic information*, was developed by Carnap and Bar-Hillel (1952). Although formally similar to information theory, the theory of semantic information is *not* information theory and differs from it in significant respects. I suggest that it is the theory of semantic information, rather than information theory, to which we should look in attempting to provide an analysis of the notion of the amount of information associated with a message.

In summary, information theory is an important mathematical tool for communication engineers and computer scientists, but it is not of much value in attempting to provide an adequate analysis of the ordinary notion of information. On most topics involved in an investigation of this notion, information theory is quite neutral; regarding the notion of the amount of information associated with a message, information theory gives results that do not conform to our pre-analytic judgments, and it does not seem amenable to changes that might bring it in line with these judgments. The semantic theory of information appears to be a more promising possibility for analyzing this notion.

3.4 INFORMATION AND UNCERTAINTY

Although information theoretic approaches have not been widely adopted by information scientists, a few have accepted one of the prominent intuitive features of this approach and used it as the basis for their own treatments of information. This feature is the thesis that information is tied to, or can be defined in terms of, uncertainty. Two such views are examined in this section, as propounded in Wersig and Neveling (1975), and Whittemore and Yovits (1973 and 1974).

The article by Wersig and Neveling is discussed in section 3.1 because it surveys the literature regarding definitions of 'information'. But Wersig and Neveling also propose their own definition, based on what they take to be the nature and role of information science. Wersig and Neveling point out that information science has its roots in the systems and technologies developed in the seventeenth and eighteenth centuries to make accessible and disseminate the fruits of the scientific revolution. As science developed, it produced an ever-greater bulk of information that needed to be arranged, stored, and made accessible. In addition, the increased number of scientists made greater demands on systems of information retrieval and dissemination.

Thus the growth of science fostered problems of great difficulty and importance involving the handling of information.

In addition, the growth and success of science had an effect on the development of society. Advanced technologies and methodologies of communication encouraged the creation of vast stores of information of all kinds and the need on the part of society to be able to access it quickly and efficiently. Information science is the discipline that deals with the problems that arise from all this. Wersig and Neveling sum up as follows:

> From a combination of historical evolution, the development of specific societal needs and the development of new methodologies and technologies, a new discipline has emerged which is sometimes called "information science." . . . This science is based on the notion of the information needs of certain people involved in social labour, and of concern with the study of methods of organization of communication processes in a way which meets these information needs (Wersig and Neveling 1975, 138).

The point stressed by Wersig and Neveling is that the main concern of information science (in their opinion) is the narrow practical problem of getting information to the people who need it.

Given this understanding of what information science is and what its goals are, Wersig and Neveling go on to argue as follows:

> The basic term 'information' can be understood only if it is defined in relation to these information needs [i.e., the information needs of people involved in social labour]
> Either as reduction of uncertainty caused by communicated data.
> Or as data used for reducing uncertainty [sic.] (Wersig and Neveling 1975, 138).

Wersig and Neveling unfortunately do not go on to further explain or justify their definition of 'information'.

In assessing the adequacy of Wersig and Neveling's position on the nature of information, the first thing to note is that their definition is extremely vague. Wersig and Neveling do not make clear what sort of a thing a "reduction of uncertainty caused by communicated data" is. If this is some sort of mental event or process, then the first disjunct of their definition makes information a process or event. The second disjunct states that information is a certain kind of data. But Wersig and Neveling never say what data is. It could be tokens, types, or something else. Presumably, whatever data is, it is not a process or event. Consequently the two disjuncts do not appear to be compatible. This may be acceptable if Wersig and Neveling mean to suggest that there are two senses of 'information', or that a choice is to be made between the two disjuncts in adopting a definition of information. Wersig and Neveling do not, however, indicate how this disjunction is to be understood.

Despite the vagueness of Wersig and Neveling's definition, it is at least clear that whatever kind of thing information might be, this kind of thing can *be* information only if it succeeds in reducing (someone's) uncertainty about something. Our criticism of Wersig and Neveling's position is therefore restricted to this claim.

In order for a message to reduce uncertainty, it must presumably be used in communication. Therefore one consequence of Wersig and Neveling's view is that something is information only if it is used in communication. This is the same restriction imposed by Farradane concerning which tokens count as information, that is, Farradane requires that a token be used in communication to count as information. In subsection 3.2.1 a counter-example to this part of Farradane's position was produced. The same story provides a counter-example to Wersig and Neveling's position. Recall that the example involves a robot spacecraft which ascertains that the atmosphere of a certain planet is fifty percent nitrogen, but is prevented from transmitting a message to that effect. The spacecraft is in possession of the information that the atmosphere of the planet is half nitrogen, but communicates this fact to no one. This shows that information can be present *without* its being used in communication, which is contrary to Wersig and Neveling's position.

The next objection concerns the claim that something counts as information only if it succeeds in *reducing* someone's uncertainty about something. The objection rests on two counter-examples, one in which it appears that information is passed from one individual to another without altering the uncertainty of the receiver whatever, and one in which it appears that in-

formation can *increase* the uncertainty of the receiver. First, suppose that Smith tells Jones that P, where Smith knows that P,
Jones doesn't know that P, and is uncertain about P, Jones understands Smith, and so on. In other words, suppose that a
straightforward instance of the communication of the fact that
P takes place. One is inclined to say that Smith informs Jones
that P, and that Smith has passed the information that P to Jones.
In short, information, whatever it is, is present in this act of
communication and gets from Smith to Jones. Now suppose
further that Jones, for whatever reason, mistrusts Smith and
doesn't believe Smith's claim that P—Jones thinks that Smith
doesn't know what he or she is talking about and simply places
no stock whatever in what Smith says. Then Jones' uncertainty
is not altered by what Smith says. Even though Smith provides
information to Jones, Jones' uncertainty is unaffected. On Wersig
and Neveling's account, if Jones' uncertainty is unaffected then
Smith *cannot* have provided information to Jones. But this example seems to indicate otherwise, showing that the requirement
that information reduce uncertainty is not part of rules governing
our use of the term 'information'.

For the second counter-example to Wersig and Neveling's position, suppose as before that Smith tells Jones that P, only now
Jones believes Smith. Suppose that before talking to Smith, Jones
was quite certain that not-P, and furthermore that Jones believed
that Q is the case only if P is the case. On the basis of these
beliefs, Jones also believed (being a good logician) that not-Q,
and in fact was quite certain that not-Q. When Smith tells Jones
that P, and Jones realizes that he or she had been holding a false
belief, Jones also realizes that he or she is no longer justified in
believing that not-Q, since not-Q does not follow from Jones'
beliefs that P and that Q only if P. (In other words, Jones does
not commit the fallacy of affirming the consequent.) Therefore,
Jones is plunged into uncertainty regarding Q. The net result of
Jones' conversation with Smith is an *increase* in Jones' uncertainty. But surely Smith has imparted information to Jones, and
possibly very valuable information at that. Hence the requirement that information reduce uncertainty cannot be correct.

Wersig and Neveling's position is very vaguely stated and
lacks any supporting evidence. Upon examination, it is found
to make only one fairly precise claim (namely that information

must reduce uncertainty), and this claim is subject to objections based on three convincing counter-examples. I conclude that Wersig and Neveling's position is inadequate as a characterization of the nature of information.

In the previous section of this chapter, a passage from Whittemore and Yovits (1973) was cited to illustrate that the information theoretic approach to information is widely thought to be inadequate to the needs of information science. In particular, Whittemore and Yovits feel that the information theoretic approach is "too restrictive to be of wide interest" (1973, 222) to information scientists. On the other hand, the authors feel that the ordinary sense of 'information', which they take to be synonymous with 'knowledge', is too broad to be of interest. They state,

> the treatment of information to be synonymous with knowledge, while this would be almost the broadest view that could be taken, appears to the authors to be far too broad to lead to principles and relationships that are meaningful and useful (Whittemore and Yovits 1973, 222).

Consequently, Whittemore and Yovits attempt to steer a middle course between the restrictiveness of the information theoretic notion of information and the breadth of the ordinary language sense of 'information'. Whittemore and Yovits are thus avowedly *not* attempting to provide an analysis of 'information' in its ordinary sense, so it is a little unfair to consider (in accord with our aims throughout this chapter) whether they have succeeded in providing such an analysis. We can, however, consider the question whether, if Whittemore and Yovits' position *were* regarded as an analysis of 'information' in its ordinary sense, it would be adequate.

Whittemore and Yovits limit their attention to the context of decision-making, which they define as "purposeful activity or intelligent behavior" (1973, 222). Under constraints regarding measurability, the need for a decision-maker to get feedback about decisions, and so on, Whittemore and Yovits develop a general model of an information system supporting a decision-maker. They stress that their model is unique in that it incorporates various kinds of uncertainty into the model of decision-making. This treatment of uncertainty paves the way for a characterization of information: any data that alters a decision-maker's uncertainty is information. In Yovits and Whittemore's model of decision-making, the uncertainty of a decision-maker at any moment is quantifiable. Hence it is possible to measure the change in uncertainty of a decision-maker upon receipt of some data, providing a measure of information.

Whittemore and Yovits' model of decision-making is quite complex. It involves six kinds of uncertainty and a rather complicated mathematical treatment of the relationships between outcomes, courses of action, utilities of various outcomes, and so forth. This seems to be why they officially define information not as data which alters the uncertainty of a decision-maker (since this uncertainty is a complicated function of the six kinds of uncertainty—a kind of "overall" uncertainty), but as "data of value in decision-making" (1973, 222). In any case, their treatment is still a species of those that treat information as something which changes uncertainty, albeit their special brand of uncertainty.

Whittemore and Yovits' treatment is mathematical and highly abstract. In order to examine in detail how well their definition of 'information' can serve as an analysis of 'information' in its everyday sense, we must connect the model with everyday discourse in some fashion, but with very little guidance as to how to do this. Rather than undertake the task of considering a series of mundane interpretations of the model, using each one as a basis for criticism, we will instead enter several objections of a more general nature that will presumably stand under any interpretation of the model.

To begin with, Whittemore and Yovits define information as a certain kind of data. Such an analysis or characterization of one thing in terms of another is called a *reductive analysis*. A reductive analysis is not objectionable in itself—on the contrary, significant theoretical advances are frequently realized by providing reductive analyses. For example, the reduction of numbers to sets and the reduction and unification of the notions of mass and energy into the composite notion of mass-energy are important instances of reductive analyses. Nevertheless, not every reductive analysis is productive or enlightening. In general, a reductive analysis of A to B is fruitful only if either (i) B is clearly understood, so that analyzing A in terms of B provides a clear understanding of A as well or (ii) B is an established and essential item in our ontology or conceptual scheme, so that reducing A to B simplifies our ontology or conceptual scheme. A reductive analysis that fails to meet either of these requirements, and thus fails to clarify or simplify our theories, has nothing to recommend it.

I suggest that Whittemore and Yovits' reductive analysis of information to data is among those reductive analyses that have nothing to recommend them. Whittemore and Yovits never say what data is. Certainly this notion, as they use it, is no clearer than the notion of information itself. Furthermore, there is no reason to believe that data is an ontological primitive, nor that the notion of data (whatever it is) is an indispensable part of our conceptual scheme. Hence Whittemore and Yovits' analysis of information fails to provide any clarification or simplification of our theories about the nature of information.

A second problem is that Whittemore and Yovits' model is built entirely in terms of decision-making. But much information give-and-take occurs purely for the sake of finding out about the world. A reader of the gossip columns is acquiring information, though presumably the data obtained has no value whatever in any decisions that person makes. Hence Whittemore and Yovits' view cannot account for a large class of activities that apparently involve information.

Whittemore and Yovits' position is also subject to a few of the counter-examples cited above against Wersig and Neveling's position. Presumably, data can be of value in decision-making only if it is conveyed to a decision-maker. Hence Whittemore and Yovits' account has the consequence that data is information only if it is used in communication with a decision-maker. The robot spacecraft example, we recall, indicates that this consequence is unacceptable if their account is to be adequate as an analysis of information.

Wersig and Neveling's position is prey to an objection in the form of a counter-example in which information serves to *increase* the uncertainty of the recipient. Whittemore and Yovits' position has the virtue of not being subject to such a counter-example, for data counts as information in their view if it *alters* uncertainty. In fact Whittemore and Yovits call information which increases uncertainty 'negative information', and stress its importance:

> *Negative information*, despite a possible connotation of the term, does represent information that is of major significance to the DM [decision-maker]. For example, a DM's initial model of the situation may have been too simplistic in that he failed to include some viable course of action. Or perhaps he mistakenly assumed that the execution of a given course of action always resulted in the same outcome. Information that caused the DM to change either of these mistaken beliefs would show up negatively . . . yet such information actually contributes to a more accurate model of the situation and is, therefore, clearly significant . . . It is clear that situations exist where information presented to us makes us *more uncertain* of our appraisal of a particular situation (Whittemore and Yovits 1973, 230).

Thus one of the counter-examples against Wersig and Neveling's account does not serve here.

The counter-example used against Wersig and Neveling in which uncertainty is *unchanged* applies against Whittemore and Yovits, however. Recall that this counter-example posits that Smith transfers information to Jones but Jones doesn't believe it. Whittemore and Yovits do not discuss the issue of whether a decision-maker makes decisions about whether to believe what he or she is told. If such choices are made, however, then it seems that the counter-example just mentioned will apply against Whittemore and Yovits' position.

In summary, Whittemore and Yovits' account of information as data of value in decision-making is lacking in several respects as an adequate analysis of 'information' in its ordinary sense. It fails to provide any simplification or clarification of the ordinary notion of information, it is too restrictive in that it considers information only in the context of decision-making, and it is subject to several counter-examples of acceptable uses of 'information' for which it fails to account. I conclude that, although Whittemore and Yovits were not attempting to provide an analysis of 'information' in its ordinary sense, their account cannot be taken as being adequate for such an analysis.

3.5 OTHER APPROACHES

To finish up this survey of discussions of the nature of information appearing in the information science literature, I consider three views that do not fit into any of the categories distinguished in the sections above. They are propounded in articles by Fairthorne (1965), Schreider (1965), and Belkin and Robertson (1976).

3.5.1 Fairthorne

Fairthorne takes terminological confusion as his topic in his 1965 article " 'Use' and 'Mention' in the Information Sciences." His premise is that while some terminological corruption is inevitable in an emerging discipline, in information science "terminological corruption has gone well beyond what is inevitable into what is scandalous" (1965, 9). One of the prime examples of corrupt terminology in information science is the term 'information' and its derivatives. The technical literature of information science has the characteristic of employing the term 'information' very frequently and in very many senses. Fairthorne elaborates on this point as follows:

> Sometimes an alert, knowledgeable, charitable, and patient reader can deduce that by "information" the author denotes "signals," "documents," "assertions," "notions," "sensations," "printed marks," and so on. Sometimes he can deduce only that the writer believes the word to be the name of a distinct self-subsistent entity or mystic essence. "Information" is not an entity, though people who use the word or are bombarded with it often enough get to believe that it is. Actually it is no more than a linguistic convenience that saves you the trouble of thinking about what you are talking about (Fairthorne 1965, 10).

When people use the term 'information' as if it refers to some sort of substance or "mystic essence," as Fairthorne says, then they are tacitly (or sometimes explicitly) subscribing to a position that Fairthorne calls the *Phlogiston Theory of Information*. Concerning this theory, Fairthorne says that it is

> analogous to the eighteenth-century theory of caloric and is equally harmful, distorting and obscuring the proper nature and targets

of the information sciences. Use of "information" as the name of
some universal essence, that can be squeezed out of texts like
water from a sponge, blurs fundamental differences such as that
between a library and a laboratory, an answer and a response, a
command and a question, a fact and a factual statement, an event
and the record of an event, and so on (Fairthorne 1965, 10).

Thus the word 'information' is used, according to Fairthorne,
either to designate something more properly and precisely referred to by other terms (like 'documents', 'signals', etc.), or, in
line with the Phlogiston Theory, to designate (paraphrasing John
Locke), "something, we know not what."

Fairthorne's recommendation is therefore that we not use the
word 'information' at all—and this goes for words derivative of
'information' as well.

Fortunately, one does not have to use the word "information."
Always, if we put our mind to it, we can say what we mean . . .
neither the noun "information" nor the verb "to inform" need be
or should be used when discussing our basic activities. If the noun
is used meaningfully, it is always better replaced by a more specific
term. The verb means no more—in the first instance—than "to
tell", "to notify", or "to communicate" in the narrowest sense
(Fairthorne 1965, 10–11).

In summary, then, Fairthorne's argument is that the term 'information' and its derivatives are overused and ill-used, pro-
moting sloppiness and confusion. In particular, the word
'information' either designates something more precisely referred to by another term, or some mystical essence, and so in
any case can only work against the goals of clarity and precision.
Hence there ought to be a moratorium on the use of 'information'
and its derivatives as a first step in cleaning up our terminology
and clarifying what we are talking about.

Fairthorne's argument is compelling and his conclusions and
recommendations very attractive. This is so particularly in light
of the fact that eighteen years have passed since the publication
of Fairthorne's article, and in this time the terminological corruption he berates has only gotten worse. However, Fairthorne
may be too sweeping in his claim that all uses of 'information'
can be eliminated all that easily. Certainly when 'information'

can be eliminated all that easily. Certainly when 'information' is used (really misused) to refer to signals, sensations, messages, and so forth, it can and should be replaced by a more precise and appropriate term. But when 'information' is used to refer to "something, we know not what," it is often the case that something important indeed *is* being said but it is not obvious how it might be said (any more clearly) without the word 'information'. Consider the following examples:

> More information is contained in the book than in the article.

> Contingent sentences contain information while tautologies do not.

> Both sentences contain the same information.

> In a deductively valid argument, the conclusion contains no more information than do the premises taken together.

These sentences are neither nonsense nor trivial, nor is it obvious how to express the claims made by these sentences in a clear way without using the term 'information'. For example, the first sentence might be rephrased as "The book says more about a certain topic than does the article." But what exactly does "saying more about a certain topic" consist in? Here the elimination of 'information' has not helped us at all.

Another way of making the same point is to note that Fairthorne is really urging that we adopt information nominalism over information realism (recall that these terms are discussed in section 1.1.5). However, Fairthorne has not even attempted to show, as every nominalist must, that the apparent ontological commitment of our talk is not real, and that we may say everything that we need to say without committing ourselves to the existence of information. Thus Fairthorne's nominalism, while attractive in principle, is far from being a defensible position.

Another objection involves Fairthorne's rather cavalier disposal of information realism. Here I do not question his refusal to countenance a mysterious "something we know not what," but to his assumption that this something can't be demystified, that 'information' does not refer to some sort of entity whose properties might be discovered through careful investigation.

In conclusion, Fairthorne's arguments and suggestions are attractive, and his position regarding the mystical nature of information may turn out to be correct. But his program for eliminating 'information' and its derivatives is seriously incomplete, and he seems too pessimistic regarding the possibility of providing an ontologically respectable (i.e., non-mystical) account of the nature of information. Hence Fairthorne's views do not constitute a sufficient reason for abandoning our task of providing an adequate analysis of 'information'.

3.5.2 Schreider

Schreider's treatment of information somewhat resembles the views that define information in terms of the change in uncertainty of a receiver considered in section 3.4, though Schreider does not make an appeal to uncertainty. Instead, Schreider's view considers the effect of received messages on something he terms a 'thesaurus'. The thesaurus θ for a receiver is a guide "in which is recorded . . . the knowledge of some receiver of information . . . about the external world" (Schreider 1965, 224). A thesaurus is thus a representation of a receiver's "belief-state" about the world. Any statement or message received, denoted T, effects a transformation of the thesaurus θ. Thus to each T corresponds a function A[T] which maps states of θ into states of θ. In other words, if θ is the thesaurus corresponding to some person's beliefs, then θ is in a certain state s_1, at some time. When a message T is received, a transformation of θ occurs, which changes the state of θ from s_1 to s_2. This corresponds to the process of learning something, or coming to have different beliefs.

On this basis Schreider introduces the following definition:

The amount of information $I(\theta,T)$ will be defined as the degree of change of the thesaurus under the action of the given statement T (Schreider 1965, 225).

Schreider then offers explanations of the conditions under which statements convey information, when they convey the same information, and so on. For example, a statement conveys information if $I(\theta,T)>0$, that is, when the statement has some effect, however slight, on the thesaurus. If the thesaurus already contains T (i.e., the receiver already believes that T) or T is not understood, then $I(\theta,T) = 0$ and T contains no information. If two statements T1 and T2 are such that $I(\theta,T1) = I(\theta,T2)$, that is, they result in changes of θ in just the same degree, then they contain the same *amount* of information, but not necessarily the *same* information. They convey the same information, or are informationally synonymous, only if the transformations A[T1] and A[T2] associated with them are identical. Thus the synonymy of statements is a matter of their leading to just the same change of state of the thesaurus. Schreider provides a formal system to go along with his informal presentation; we need not consider it, however.

Schreider's position has a great deal of mathematical elegance, but it is subject to two serious objections that render it quite useless in the investigation of information. First, Schreider's view has the shortcoming that it deals with information conveyed by a message, but not with information contained in, or transferred by, a message. These notions are too important to be neglected in any analysis of the ordinary notion of information.

A more serious objection to Schreider's position is that it offers an empty formalism without contributing anything of value to our investigation of information. For example, consider the claim that the statement T conveys information to some individual if $I(\theta,T)>0$. Schreider considers this to be an important consequence of his account. However, when we unravel the formalism, this claim amounts to the truism that a statement T conveys information to some individual if the individual understands T and changes his or her belief-state on the basis of T. This is hardly surprising. Furthermore, it is not derived from other parts of Schreider's position in an insightful or elegant fashion, so its derivation is not enlightening either. This commonplace is merely restated in Schreider's formal idiom, apparently simply for the sake of stating it in the formal idiom.

There are important and difficult questions surrounding Schreider's position, questions whose answers would constitute significant advances in our understanding of information. For example, the central notion in Schreider's account is that of a thesaurus. Schreider tells us that a thesaurus represents a person's belief-state, but he never indicates, even vaguely, how a thesaurus does this. Yet this is one of the crucial questions for any position that claims to model human cognitive processes.

To take another example, Schreider posits a function that takes statements as arguments and works transformations on a thesaurus. Yet Schreider never gives any indication of how this function works. It is quite fruitless to posit a rule-governed transformation without indicating, at least in outline, the rules involved. After all, we already know that statements conveyed to an individual alter his or her belief-states in a fairly predictable and regular fashion—the question is, what are the rules governing this process? Schreider never addresses this question.

Schreider's position is clear, simple, and precise, and to that extent it is quite attractive. However, it neglects important aspects of the notion of information by failing to consider the information contained and transferred by messages. Even more seriously, the elegant formal model that Schreider propounds is quite empty thanks to its tenuous connection with the phenomena it pretends to represent. Schreider fails to consider any of the difficult questions concerning the nature of the entities and processes that he claims to be modeling, and consequently he produces no helpful or enlightening results.

3.5.3 Belkin and Robertson

Probably the most sophisticated approach to the problem of determining the nature of information that has appeared in the information science literature, is that of Belkin and Robertson (1976). Belkin and Robertson start with a notion we've already encountered in this chapter, that of an image, in Boulding's (1956) sense. They describe an image as "the mental conception that we have of our environment and ourselves in it" (Belkin and Robertson [1976], 198). Images have *structure*, where

structure should be regarded as a category, rather than a concept; that is, it is of universal applicability (in a sense, everything has structure) (Belkin and Robertson 1976, 198).

This does little to explain what "structure" means, but Belkin and Robertson continue their argument without further explanation. I will have more to say about the notion of structure presently.

Belkin and Robertson state that when they consider how 'information' is used, they can find nothing common to all uses except the idea of structures being changed.

> We are therefore tempted to define [information] as follows:
> *Information is that which is capable of transforming structure*
> This definition, however, is clearly far too broad (particularly in view of the categorical nature of structure), and encompasses many notions for which the term information is never used. So we leave information (in its general sense) undefined; but we discuss the various uses of the term with the idea of transforming of structure in mind (Belkin and Robertson 1976, 198).

Belkin and Robertson thus seem to be arguing that there is not, and cannot be, a definition of 'information' in its general sense. Consequently, they take as their goal a definition of 'information' as the word is used just in the field of information science.

To achieve this goal, Belkin and Robertson must of course decide what the field of information science is. Consciously modeling their description on Wersig and Neveling (1975) (see section 3.4), Belkin and Robertson define 'information science' as the purpose-oriented discipline which aims to "facilitate the communication of information between human beings" (1976, 200). Belkin and Robertson next survey "a wide spectrum of information concepts [that] are in current use, in a variety of disciplines" (1976, 198). They find that a portion of this spectrum can be singled out as particularly germane to the needs and interests of information science. Furthermore,

> that part of the spectrum which we have indicated as being of interest to information science is characterized by: the *deliberate* (*purposeful*) structuring of the message by the sender in order to *affect* the image structure of the recipient (Belkin and Robertson 1976, 200).

Belkin and Robertson claim to have thus shown that there is a "unique concept of information specific to the needs and purposes of information science" (1976, 201).

Finally, Belkin and Robertson present their definition of "the basic concepts of information science" based on the above argument:

> A TEXT (*in information science*) is a collection of signs purposefully structured by a sender with the intention of changing the image-structure of a recipient. INFORMATION (*in information science*) is the structure of any text which is capable of changing the image-structure of a recipient (Belkin and Robertson 1976, 201).

The virtue of these definitions is that they make clear distinctions between things not distinguished in most other characterizations of information in information science. For example, the *carrier* of information (text) is distinguished from the information. Also, information is separated from the *effect* its communication may or may not have (i.e., the possible change in image-structure of a recipient). Unfortunately there are several features of Belkin and Robertson's position that make it unsuitable as an analysis of 'information'.

Before proceeding with my criticisms, it must in fairness be stressed that Belkin and Robertson do not claim to supply an adequate analysis of 'information' in its ordinary sense. However, as in previous similar cases, we may still consider, in line with the overall goal of this chapter, whether their position *could* serve as such an analysis.

The most troublesome feature of Belkin and Robertson's view is that it defines 'information' in terms of 'structure', but then fails to make clear what the latter term refers to. Besides the rather opaque passage already cited, Belkin and Robertson also claim concerning 'structure' that they "assume *structure* to be understood in its most general form as *order*" (Belkin and Robertson 1976, 201). This is unenlightening and furthermore suggests an interpretation of their definitions that Belkin and Robertson presumably do not intend. For if information is the *order* of a text, and a text is an *ordered* collection of symbols, then information is the *order* of the symbols appearing in a collection of symbols. Then the information in a text changes if a few words are juxtaposed. For example, the information in the text "The ball is round and blue" would be different from that in the text "The ball is blue and round," which is obviously incorrect.

Belkin and Robertson must be faulted for replacing one mystery by another in their definition of 'information', leading to the conclusion that their position is unacceptable at least on the grounds of clarity.

Another major difficulty with Belkin and Robertson's position arises from its two-fold requirement that (1) information be associated with a text and (2) a text be generated by a sender with certain *intentions*. Counter-examples to this requirement are easily generated. For example, suppose X keeps a diary as a form of therapy or self-analysis, with no intention whatever of letting anyone see it, or even of rereading it at some later time. Then X has no intention of changing the image-structure of a recipient, so the diary is not a text. But if it is not a text, then it has, or contains, no information. The diary, however, obviously contains information, so the above two-fold requirement cannot be correct. We conclude that Belkin and Robertson fail on the grounds of ordinary use, as well as on ontological grounds, to supply an adequate analysis of 'information' in its ordinary sense.

3.6 CONCLUSION

This completes our review of the information science literature regarding the nature of information. I have shown that information science lacks an accepted view of the nature of information, despite the fact that many proposals have been made in this regard. Furthermore, I have argued that these proposals all fail, in one way or another, to adequately represent the ordinary notion of information. In the next chapter I begin to present my own analysis of information, taking up the discussion of the ontological nature of information left off at the end of Chapter 2.

4
INFORMATION AND PROPOSITIONS

The last two chapters have focused on what information is not; the present chapter makes a proposal regarding what information is. Specifically, I propose in this chapter that information be analyzed in terms of propositions. However, a complete analysis or explication of propositions will not be attempted in this work. My aim is rather to show that given a reasonably clear notion of propositions, we can arrive at a satisfactory analysis of information in terms of propositions.

An analysis of information in terms of propositions is a reductive analysis. In section 3.4 it was suggested that a reductive analysis of A to B is worthwhile only if at least one of two conditions is met, namely that either (i) B is clearly understood, so that analyzing A in terms of B gains us a clear understanding of A or (ii) B is required in our ontology or conceptual scheme, so that analyzing A in terms of B simplifies our ontology or conceptual scheme.

I submit that the reduction of information to propositions meets both of these conditions. As Chapter 3 demonstrates, information is not well understood. Propositions, however, are much better understood, due largely to the fact that propositions have been under philosophical scrutiny for hundreds of years. It cannot be claimed that propositions are *perfectly* well understood; propositions have been, and remain, the subject of philosophical debate precisely because they are not as well understood as we would like. Nonetheless, centuries of discussion have resulted in some progress toward a satisfactory account of the nature of propositions, so we stand to gain much ground if information can be analyzed in terms of propositions. Hence such an analysis, if it can be accomplished, would be worthwhile according to the first criterion enumerated above.

In addition, a successful analysis of information in terms of propositions would simplify our ontology and conceptual scheme. Propositions serve an essential role in our theories as bearers of truth-values and as objects of propositional attitudes (more on this below). If information can be eliminated in terms of propositions (which we need anyway), the result is a simplification of our ontology. For if information is propositions, then we do not posit two sorts of things (propositions *and* information), but one sort of thing (propositions) which, under the appropriate circumstances, we call information. Hence the successful reduction of information to propositions meets the second as well as the first condition of adequacy mentioned above, and so would be an advance in our theories of the nature of information.

4.1 THE PROPOSITIONAL APPROACH

The suggestion that information be understood in terms of propositions (or some other semantic entity) is not entirely absent from the information science literature. In a recent article, Patrick Wilson (1978) takes a step in this direction. Wilson first considers whether information might be sentence tokens or sentence types (the text of a document) and marshals the same arguments as in Chapter 2 against this position. He concludes that

> The information contained in a document cannot be identified with the text of the document. But it may be identified with the sense, meaning, propositional content, or semantic content of the text (Wilson 1978, 11).

Wilson notes that these four things are not necessarily the same, but then he unfortunately takes his discussion of this point no further, preferring to focus on the process of interpreting a document's text.

Although Wilson's comment does not take us very far in our investigation, it does prompt us to note several important points about providing an analysis of information in terms of propositions. First, it is important to be as clear as possible about what propositions are, and in particular how they are related to meanings. Second, besides providing arguments in favor of analyzing information in terms of propositions, it should be clear why propositions are to be preferred over closely related things, like meanings. The next few subsections address these issues. In the first two subsections, I clarify the notion of a proposition by contrasting it first with sentences, then with meanings. The third subsection contains arguments in favor of analyzing information in terms of propositions, and the fourth offers an argument against analyzing information as meaning.

4.1.1 Propositions and Sentences

There are many ways of approaching the notion of a proposition, but for our purposes it is useful to begin by contrasting propositions with sentences. Consider the sentence

A. Mars has two moons.

In light of our discussion in Chapter 2, we can distinguish the sentence type of A from the sentence token A. We may, however, further distinguish the *proposition* expressed by A, which is *what is asserted to be the case by (someone who writes or utters) A*, namely that Mars has two moons.

I mention the type/token distinction in order to contrast propositions with both sentence tokens and sentence types. With regard to sentence tokens, recall that a sentence token is a spatio-temporal object which occurs at a particular place and at a particular time or over some duration of time. What is asserted, however, is not a spatio-temporal entity. That Mars has two moons is not the sort of thing that occurs at a particular place and time. Such considerations do not apply to propositions. To further illustrate this point, consider the inscription

B. Mars has two moons.

Since A and B are distinct inscriptions, they are distinct sentence tokens. However, both express the proposition that Mars has two moons. Therefore propositions cannot be sentence tokens.

In fact propositions are atemporal and non-spatial; they are abstract objects, like sets, numbers, or sentence types. Propositions are distinct from these other sorts of things, though; in particular, they are distinct from sentence types, as can be established by the following argument. Consider these sentences

C.   Two moons circle Mars.

D.   The number of moons of Mars is the first prime number.

E.   Mars a deux lunes.

In Chapter 2, it was pointed out that two sentence types S and T are identical only if the sequence of word types associated with any token of S is the same as the sequence of word types associated with any token of T. Hence B, C, D, and E are tokens of distinct sentence types. However, all represent the world as being the same way—all express the same proposition. Hence propositions must be distinct from sentence types.

Another, similar argument is based on indexical sentences. Consider the sentence

F. Mars has two of them.

In the appropriate contexts, this single sentence type (or instances of it) can be used to assert any number of distinct propositions, as, for example, that Mars has two moons, or two poles, or two canals, or two inhabitants, and so on. Thus we see that in general the identity conditions for propositions are quite different from those for sentence types. (Since subsequent discussion involves sentence types almost exclusively, the reader may assume that hereafter, whenever sentences are mentioned, sentence *types* are being referred to.)

Although propositions are distinct from sentences they are nonetheless systematically associated with sentences, particularly indicative sentences. This is because in making claims about the world we typically employ indicative sentences. But a claim about the world is a proposition. Hence indicative sentences are used to *express* propositions. For example, the indicative sentence 'Mars has two moons' is used to express the proposition that Mars has two moons.

Besides expressing propositions, indicative sentences are also employed in the conventional method for naming propositions. A proposition may be named or designated by a *that*-clause, where a "*that*-clause" is formed by concatenating the word 'that' and an indicative sentence. The proposition named by the *that*-clause is the proposition expressed by the indicative sentence employed in the *that*-clause. So, for example, the *that*-clause 'that Mars has two moons' names the proposition expressed by the sentence 'Mars has two moons', that is, the proposition that Mars has two moons (more on this in section 4.1.3).

Shortly we will have occasion to introduce variables standing for sentences and propositions. To mark the distinction between the two, we adopt the convention that lowercase letters are to stand for propositions, and uppercase letters are to stand for sentences. Furthermore, propositions and *that*-clauses used to name them are to employ the same letter. Thus the proposition referred to by the *that*-clause 'that P' is p.

Propositions have traditionally been called on to play several different roles, three of which are particularly important in this essay. The first such traditional role for propositions is as the bearers of truth-values, things which are susceptible of truth or falsity. This is because a proposition is supposed to represent the world as being a certain way. Clearly, something that represents the world as being a certain way is faithful to the facts or not. If the former, then the proposition is true; if the latter, it is false. Thus propositions are the sort of thing (and, many have maintained, the primary or only sort of thing) that bears truth-values.

A second important traditional role of propositions is as the objects of certain mental states, called the *propositional attitudes*. Propositional attitudes are designated by verbs, called *propositional verbs*, which take *that*-clauses as complements and refer to various "mental states". Examples of such verbs are 'know', 'think', 'believe', 'suspect', 'doubt', and so forth. In many accounts of propositional attitudes, the attitude is taken to be a relation between an agent and a proposition. Thus, for example, my belief that Mars has two moons is taken to be a relation between me and the proposition that Mars has two moons. As such, propositions are said to be the "objects" of these relations and of the corresponding attitudes. The apparent objectual status of propositions with respect to the propositional attitudes, notably knowing and believing, will figure prominently in later discussion.

The third traditional role of propositions is as the meanings of indicative sentences. If propositions are the meanings of sentences, then the important semantic relations of likeness and difference of meaning (of sentences) may be easily explained in terms of the identity or difference of the propositions expressed by sentences. Thus propositions have frequently been employed as major theoretical entities in semantic theories.

I believe that propositions are quite miscast in the role of the meanings of sentences. Since this question is important for our analysis, the next section is devoted to defending the claim that propositions are not the meanings of (indicative) sentences.

4.1.2 Propositions and Meaning

In order to make the case that propositions are not the meanings of sentences it is necessary to bring out a subtle but very important distinction masked by various common locutions involving the words 'mean' and 'meaning'. In particular, it is necessary to be quite clear about what is *not* covered by the phrase 'the meaning of a sentence' in this instance, and hence what is not comprehended by my claim that propositions are not the meanings of sentences.

Two locutions involving the word 'mean' have already figured prominently (in section 1.1.3) in distinguishing between what a person's words mean (on some occasion) and what a person means in using certain words (on some occasion). To recall this distinction, suppose that X, in Syracuse, New York, remarks to a friend

A. It's always so sunny here!

meaning, of course, that it is not very sunny at all in Syracuse. Then what the *person* X means in using A on that occasion, namely that Syracuse is not sunny, may be distinguished from what X's *words* (the sentence A) mean on that occasion, namely that Syracuse is sunny. For brevity, I hereafter refer to the former construal of the phrase 'the meaning of S' as the 'meaning$_1$ of S', and the latter construal as the 'meaning$_2$ of S'.

Note that both meaning$_1$ and meaning$_2$ are "occasion-sensitive" in the sense that both the meaning$_1$ and the meaning$_2$ of a sentence may change as the occasion of use of the sentence changes. For example, someone in Sun City, Arizona may use sentence A with both meaning$_1$ and meaning$_2$ that Sun City is sunny. Then the meaning$_1$ and the meaning$_2$ of A have changed just by virtue of a change in the occasion of use of the sentence. Clearly, even eternal sentences have varying meanings$_1$, and there is no limit whatever to the number of both meanings$_1$ and meanings$_2$ that indexical sentences may have.

In contrast to the occasion-sensitivity exhibited by the meaning$_1$ and meaning$_2$ of sentences, there is an important sense in which the meanings of sentences do *not* change with the occasion of their use. This is the sense in virtue of which it is intelligible to claim, for example, that a sentence has *one* meaning no matter whether it is used in Syracuse, Sun City, or Siberia. Richard Cartwright makes this point as follows:

Consider the words 'It's raining'. These are words, in the uttering of which, people often (though not always) assert something. But of course *what* is asserted varies from one occasion of their utterance to another. A person who utters them one day does not (normally) make the same statement as one who utters them the next; and one who utters them in Oberlin does not usually assert what is asserted by one who utters them in Detroit. But these variations in what is asserted are *not* accompanied by corresponding changes in meaning. The words 'It's raining' retain the same meaning throughout. Words do sometimes change their meaning . . . And it *may* be that the words 'It's raining' have come to mean something other than what they once meant. We can at least imagine that they should in the future come to have a different meaning, so that (say) they come to be appropriate only for steady downpours, not for drizzles or cloudbursts. Similarly, some words

mean one thing in one locality and another in another . . . And
we can imagine that the words 'It's raining' should be subject to
some such regional variation in usage. All this is sensible enough.
But it is surely ridiculous to suggest that the words 'It's raining'
change in meaning from week to week, from day to day, from
one moment to the next—and this only because of a change in
time; and how astounding would it be were their meaning to
change with *every* change in place—and this for *no* other reason
than that the place had changed (Cartwright 1962, 92).

Let us designate this invariant sort of meaning of a sentence S
the 'meaning$_0$ of S'.

The meaning$_0$ of a sentence S is fixed by the syntactic and
semantic rules of English, not by the variable features of context.
As such, it is the meaning$_0$ of a sentence that enables us, given
the necessary contextual factors, to fix the meaning$_1$ and meaning$_2$
of the sentence on some occasion (more on this below). Hence
the meaning$_0$ of a sentence S has primacy over the meanings$_1$
and meanings$_2$ of S.

Furthermore, it is the meaning$_0$ of sentences that is involved
in most of the claims we commonly make about the meanings
of sentences. Usually, claims about the meanings of sentences
(as opposed to claims about what is *meant* by a sentence) are
about the sameness or difference of meaning of sentences, and
it is only the meanings$_0$ of sentences that count in making such
determinations. To illustrate, consider the following sentences:

B.   We're all bozos on this bus.

C.   Everyone on this bus is a bozo.

D.   We're not all bozos on this bus.

I suggest that most native speakers of English would agree that
sentences B and C have the same meaning, and that this meaning
differs from the meaning of sentence D. Such an assessment is
correct only if the "sort" of meaning involved is meaning$_0$. For
on various occasions, the meanings$_1$ and meanings$_2$ of sentences
B, C, and D may be such as to make the above claims about the
sameness and difference of meaning of these sentences incorrect.

The root of all this complication is that various locutions involving the words 'mean' and 'meaning' are not as closely related as one might expect. Typically, what is understood to be the *meaning* of a sentence (i.e., the meaning$_0$) is very different from what a *person* means in using the sentence (the meaning$_1$) and from what the *sentence* means (the meaning$_2$), on some occasion. Hence in discussing "the meaning of a sentence" it is necessary that we clearly understand whether it is the "basic" or "non-contextual" notion of meaning (meaning$_0$) or one of the "extended" or "contextual" notions of meaning (meaning$_1$ or meaning$_2$), which is under discussion.

In light of this it must be stated that my claim that propositions are not the meanings of sentences is a claim regarding the meanings$_0$ of sentences, not a claim about the meanings$_1$ or meanings$_2$ of sentences.

The argument[†] that propositions are not the meanings of sentences proceeds by demonstrating that many of the characteristic or definitive features of propositions are not features of meanings of sentences, and that therefore the two cannot be identical.

When the notion of a proposition was introduced in section 4.1.1 it was characterized as being what is asserted when an assertion is made. Hence an important (and perhaps the essential) feature of propositions is that they can be asserted. Meanings of sentences, however, cannot be asserted. Consider the following sentences (following standard practice, I mark unacceptable sentences with a *):

E.   He asserted the proposition quite forcefully.

F.   *He asserted the meaning quite forcefully.

Sentence E is perfectly acceptable, but sentence F is nonsense. Meanings, like pillows, numbers, and arthritis, are simply not the sorts of things that can be asserted. Consequently, propositions cannot be the meanings of sentences.

[†] This argument is based on a similar argument for the same conclusion in Cartwright (1962, 92–102).

Propositions may be ascribed a variety of other properties besides assertability. Specifically, in their role as bearers of truth-values, propositions can be ascribed truth or falsity; in their role as objects of propositional attitudes, propositions can be described as being believable, unthinkable, certain, doubtful, and so on. However, it makes no sense to ascribe any of these properties to the meanings of sentences. For example, the meaning of a sentence cannot be true or false, nor can it be believable, unthinkable, certain, or doubtful. Hence propositions cannot be the meanings of sentences.

Cartwright, in his statement of this argument, gives an even longer list of properties that apply to propositions but not to the meanings of sentences:

> Just as the meanings of sentences cannot be asserted, neither can they be affirmed, denied, contradicted, questioned, challenged, discounted, confirmed, supported, verified, withdrawn, repudiated; and whereas what is asserted can be said to be accurate, exaggerated, unfounded, overdrawn, probable, improbable, plausible, true or false, none of these can be said of the meaning of a sentence (Cartwright 1962, 101).

In conclusion, the evidence of ordinary use is that propositions are different sorts of things from meanings, with very different properties and characteristics. Therefore propositions are distinct from the meanings of sentences.

4.1.3 The Propositional Analysis of Information

Having introduced and discussed the notion of a proposition, I am now in a position to state and defend what I will call the *propositional analysis of information*. (The analysis presented in the next few lines is tentative and is developed more fully throughout this chapter and in Chapter 9). The main tenet of this analysis is that information is propositions, or more precisely, that

> The *information* carried by a sentence S is a proposition appropriately associated with S.

In this subsection and the next, this analysis is defended on ontological grounds. I first show that information has most of the essential characteristics of propositions, and then that it is distinct from meaning. The succeeding section elaborates the analysis with respect to the "association" between information, propositions, and sentences alluded to above.

I begin the defense of my analysis by noting a close similarity in the arguments employed above on the one hand to show that information is neither sentence tokens nor sentence types, and on the other to show that propositions are neither sentence tokens nor sentence types. In both cases, the arguments against the identification of propositions and information with sentence tokens proceeded by showing that the former are atemporal and non-spatial abstract objects, while the latter are spatio-temporal objects. Likewise, the arguments against the identification of propositions and information with sentence types in both cases employed the fact that the identity conditions of the latter do not coincide with the identity conditions of the former. A review of these discussions will show that the reasoning and examples are virtually interchangeable.

These similarities lend credence to the identification of information and propositions in the following ways: first, they point out that both information and propositions are of like ontological category, namely abstract objects but not sentence types. Second, they provide an argument by analogy that propositions and information are identical. This argument is admittedly not very strong, but at least it lends credibility to the claim. Stronger arguments in justification of this claim are based on the main features and characteristics of information and propositions.

Propositions were characterized as embodying claims about the way the world is, about what is the case; propositions represent the world as being a certain way. But information does the same. Recall that we distinguished (in section 1.1.4) between information-how and information-that, and furthermore that the discussion in this study was limited to the latter. We characterized information-that as "information to the effect that some state of affairs obtains." In other words, our concern in this essay is to investigate the sort of information that embodies claims about what is the case. (We might have described information-that as "propositional information," had we a clear notion of the adjective 'propositional', for this is just the sort of information we are concerned with.) Information-that and propositions thus both embody claims about the way the world is. Hence they are either identical or there are two distinct things, both being what is said when claims about the world are made. It seems most plausible that what is said is just one thing, and hence that information is identical with propositions.

We remarked above that an important characteristic of propositions is that they are bearers of truth-values. However, information is also apparently susceptible of truth and falsity. (Detailed consideration of whether this appearance is real, and particularly of whether false information *is* information, is deferred until Chapter 9. For now, we rely only on the fact that ordinary language sanctions predications of truth and falsity to information.) For example, the following are acceptable English sentences which appear to predicate truth and falsity of information:

The information is true, but misleading.

He is accused of providing false and misleading information to consumers.

I provided information which was neither false nor misleading.

Information systems should deliver true information, though in practice they frequently deliver false information.

It is plausible that more than one sort of thing can bear truth-values. For example it has been argued that beliefs and sentences, as well as propositions, are susceptible of truth and falsity, though these three are apparently different kinds of things. Hence it may be that information and propositions are distinct, despite both being susceptible of truth and falsity. However the fact that both do bear truth-value provides circumstantial evidence in favor of the propositional analysis.

It was also noted in our discussion of propositions that they are expressed by indicative sentences. In like fashion, information-that is carried by indicative sentences. This lends further credence to the claim that information is propositions.

The next argument is based on the fact that both propositions and information are named by *that*-clauses. Suppose we wish to refer to the proposition expressed by the sentence

A.   Venus has no moon.

The most straightforward way of doing so is to use the expression

B.   the proposition that Venus has no moon.

Similarly, the information carried by sentence A can be referred to as

C.   the information that Venus has no moon.

Now consider that when we refer to a thing by means of an expression of the form "the X n" (where X is a predicate), then n must be a name for the entity in question. To illustrate this rule, note the following phrases:

the writer Truman Capote

the novelist John Updike

the actress Meryl Streep

the labor leader Douglas Fraser

In each case the expression following the predicate is a name of the entity in question. Hence when we refer to a proposition as in B, the *that*-clause

D.   that Venus has no moon

must be a name of the proposition in question. Likewise, given phrase C, the same *that*-clause must name the information referred to by C. In short, the *that*-clause D names both the proposition that Venus has no moon *and* the information that Venus has no moon. Generalizing, we see that the phrase 'that P' names both the information that P and the proposition that P. But 'that P' presumably names only one thing, so the information that P must be identical with the proposition that P. In conclusion, information is propositions.

The final argument in defense of the propositional analysis of information is based on the claim that propositions are the objects of propositional attitudes. In other words, propositions are the objects of mental or cognitive states like belief, knowledge, doubt, certainty, and so forth. Information, however, seems likewise to be capable of being the object of propositional attitudes. For example, the following sentences are legitimate:

I don't doubt your information, but it may be irrelevant.

Nixon was aware of that information.

He is certain of his information.

John believed his information.

From the grammatical structure of these sentences, it appears that information can be the object of propositional attitudes. Since propositions are supposed to be the objects of propositional attitudes, we conclude that information is propositions.

I now consider an objection against the propositional analysis of information. The objection concerns the difference between mass nouns and mass noun phrases, and count nouns and count noun phrases, so first we review this distinction.

There are nouns and noun phrases in English that designate things that can be counted. For example, chairs, people, mahogany tables, sick hamsters, and electric toasters can be counted. Nouns and noun phrases that designate such things, (like 'chair', 'person', 'mahogany table', 'sick hamster', and 'electric toaster') are called *count nouns* and *count noun phrases*. In contrast, there are other things in the world that can't be counted. Examples are liquids like water and milk, particulate matter like sugar, flour, and salt, and other sorts of stuff like electricity, air, furniture, junk, and garbage. Nouns and noun phrases designating such things (like 'milk', 'dirty water', 'mahogany furniture', and 'choice garbage') are called *mass nouns* and *mass noun phrases*.

A quick and easy test for distinguishing mass noun phrases from count noun phrases makes use of the facts that (i) it makes sense to prefix 'much' to mass noun phrases but not to count noun phrases, and (ii) it makes sense to prefix 'many' to count noun phrases but not to mass noun phrases. Thus, to distinguish count noun phrases from mass noun phrases, we need only consider whether prefixing the noun phrase with 'much' or 'many' produces anomaly. To illustrate, consider the following phrases:

* much MacIntosh apples

many MacIntosh apples

much hysterical laughter

* many hysterical laughters

It is clear from these examples that 'MacIntosh apples' is a count noun phrase while 'hysterical laughter' is a mass noun phrase.

The distinction between mass noun phrases and count noun phrases has several rather obvious grammatical consequences, the chief one being that it makes sense to predicate numerical properties of things designated by count noun phrases, but not of things designated by mass noun phrases:

There are four chairs in this room.

* There are four furnitures in this room.

The cat ate three hamsters.

* The cat ate three garbages.

There are also some sticky problems regarding the semantics of mass noun phrases which we will not consider.[†]

Now to the objection. If information is propositions, then the same properties should be predicable of both. But 'information'

[†] See Pelletier (1974) for a discussion of these problems and a critical review of their literature.

is a mass noun and 'proposition' is a count noun, as the following phrases indicate:

much information

*many informations

*much propositions

many propositions

Since 'information' and 'proposition' differ grammatically in this way there are some properties predicable of one not predicable of the other; in particular, it makes sense to predicate numerical properties of propositions but not of information. Consider the following:

The lecturer listed five propositions.

*The lecturer listed five informations.

Since the same properties are not predicable of both information and propositions, the two must be distinct.

In reply to this objection, I argue that it turns on certain peculiarities of our use of mass noun phrases that have no significant ontological consequences. Furthermore, the objection can be cleared up simply by our being more precise in stating claims regarding the relationship between information and propositions. In order to make this reply plausible, I first consider a parallel but simpler case involving a similar apparent difficulty arising from the grammar of count noun phrases and mass noun phrases.

Suppose someone were to suggest that water is hydrogen oxide molecules. Since it is quickly verified that 'water' is a mass noun and 'hydrogen oxide molecule' is a count noun phrase, it might be objected (as above) that water cannot be hydrogen oxide molecules because the same properties cannot be predicated of these two things; in particular, numerical properties can be predicated of hydrogen oxide molecules but not of water.

Thus the claim that water is hydrogen oxide molecules must be false.

Since it is common knowledge that water is made up of hydrogen oxide molecules, there is some confusion here, but not one that arises from a mistake in ontology. Rather, the problem arises from peculiarities of our use of mass noun phrases (the same peculiarities, in fact, that make it so difficult to give an adequate semantics for mass noun phrases—see Pelletier [1974]), and it may be resolved by a more precise statement of the claim in question. Consider the following:

Any body of water is (made up of) hydrogen oxide molecules.

Since the phrase 'body of water' is a count noun phrase rather than a mass noun phrase, the objection dissolves.

In like fashion, the objection against the propositional analysis of information is based on peculiarities of the grammar of mass nouns and is not of any ontological consequence. In addition, the objection is easily refuted when the analysis is more precisely and fully stated. The bare claim that information is propositions apparently falls prey to the objection. However, this claim may be restated as follows:

Any item or piece of information is (made up of) propositions.

When stated in this fashion, the analysis is immune to the objection, for the phrase 'item or piece of information' is a count noun phrase. Thus, the fact that 'information' is a mass noun while 'proposition' is a count noun does not result in the downfall of the propositional analysis of information.

On the other hand, the fact that 'information' is a mass noun does necessitate further refinement of the propositional analysis on account of two special features of mass noun phrases. Generally, mass noun phrases

have the property of *collectiveness*—they are true of any sum of the things of which they are true; and of *divisiveness*—they are true of any part (down to a certain limit) of things of which they are true (Pelletier 1974, 87).

For example, the mass noun phrase 'new-mown hay' has collectiveness because if it is true of one pile of stuff A and also of another pile of stuff B, then it is true also of the big pile of stuff formed when A and B are put together. This phrase also has divisiveness because if one takes any part of a pile of new-mown hay (down to the blades of hay) one still has new-mown hay.

The mass noun 'information' also has collectiveness and divisiveness. Several pieces of information may be combined to form a single piece of information; contrarywise a single piece of information may be divided up to form several pieces of information. We must be able to account for this in the propositional analysis of information. In doing so, however, we will have to broaden the analysis. As it now stands, the propositional analysis speaks only of the information associated with a single sentence. But the phenomena of joining and splitting information involve entire texts or sets of sentences. Consequently, we now consider how the propositional analysis of information can be extended to cover sets of sentences.

Suppose that several sentences carry a single piece of information. What is this information? It is not the information that the world is the way any *one* of the sentences (if asserted) claim it to be, though this is *part* of the information they jointly carry. Rather, it is the information to the effect that the world is the way these sentences (if asserted) *jointly* represent it to be. But the way that a set of sentences (if asserted) jointly represent the world to be is a representation of a way the world is, that is, a proposition. Specifically, it is the proposition which is the conjunction of the propositions expressed by the sentences taken individually.

Let us call the proposition consisting of the conjunction of the propositions expressed by the elements of a set $ of sentences the *conglomerate proposition* expressed by $. Then we can reformulate the propositional analysis as follows:

> The *information* carried by a set $ of sentences is the proposition
> p, where p is the conglomerate proposition expressed by a set $'
> of sentences appropriately associated with $.

This emended version of the propositional analysis of information allows us to account for the collectiveness and divisiveness of 'information' easily and elegantly. Regarding the property of collectiveness, it is clear that several distinct items of information, which are conglomerate propositions, can be combined into a single piece of information by conjoining the conglomerate propositions in question to form a single conglomerate proposition. With respect to the property of divisiveness, a single piece of information, which is a conglomerate proposition, may be divided into several pieces of information by breaking apart the larger conglomerate proposition into several of its conjuncts. Of course, if a conglomerate proposition consists of but a single "atomic" conjunct, then it cannot be broken down. However the property of divisiveness does not require that the mass noun phrase in question be true of *every* part of a thing of which it is true—only of every part *down to a certain limit*. Hence, just as a body of water can be broken down into parts that are still water only as far as the molecular level, so a piece of information can be broken down into parts which are still information only as far as the level of "atomic" propositions.

A final remark with respect to the collectiveness and divisiveness of 'information' is that these properties of the term allow us a great deal of flexibility in the ways that we may describe information. For example, we may say that a given text contains some information, or several pieces of information, or a single piece of information. Typically, we take advantage of this flexibility to bring attention to various important features of the information we are dealing with. For example, if a paragraph makes several important points, we may bring this out by saying that it contains several pieces of information. If our interest is more global, then we may refer to a paragraph or even a whole book as a single piece of information. In discussing information systems, for example, we often refer to entire documents as "information items." These aspects of usage do not, however, disturb our conclusions about the use of the term 'information'.

This completes the initial presentation and defense of the propositional analysis of information. In conclusion, it must be admitted that a staunch opponent of the propositional analysis could maintain that there really are two sorts of things that bear truth-values, are expressed by indicative sentences, are named by that-clauses, are the objects of propositional attitudes, and whose essence is to represent the world as being a certain way. However, in the absence of any arguments in favor of such a position, it appears wholly untenable, and the propositional analysis quite reasonable.

4.1.4 Information and Meaning

In section 4.1.2 I argued extensively against the thesis that propositions are the meanings of indicative sentences. To further establish the propositional analysis of information, and for its own sake as well, I argue in this section the thesis that information is likewise not the meaning of indicative sentences. This raises the question of just what the connection between meaning and information is, however. Consequently the section concludes with a few paragraphs concerning this connection.

Not surprisingly (in light of the propositional analysis of information), the argument by which it is established that propositions are not the meanings of sentences is easily recast to show that information is not the meanings of sentences. The major premise of the argument is that if information is the meaning of sentences, then anything it makes sense to say of information, it ought to make sense to say of meaning, barring statements concerning "amounts" of information and meaning. The proviso is necessary because 'information' is a mass noun and 'meaning' a count noun (at least in its use in the phrase 'the meaning of a sentence'). Consequently, differences in the grammar of these words are bound to arise on this score. However, since we have seen in the preceding section that such differences do not carry any ontological weight, they clearly ought not count against the identification of information and the meaning of sentences.

Even restricting attention to statements not having to do with amount of information and meaning, however, there are many things that may be said of information that may not intelligibly be said of the meanings of sentences, as the following examples illustrate:

The information contained in that sentence is incorrect.

*The meaning of that sentence is incorrect.

That information is quite misleading.

* That meaning is quite misleading.

The court discounted John's information.

* The court discounted John's meaning.

This list could be easily extended, and a good guide in its extension is the list of terms quoted from Cartwright in the preceeding section as applying to propositions but not to meanings. For, in general, anything it makes sense to say of information it makes sense to say of propositions, but it is *not* the case that anything it makes sense to say of propositions and information, it makes sense to say of meaning. Thus we conclude that information cannot be the meanings of sentences, just as propositions cannot be the meanings of sentences, and for just the same reason.

Information is not meaning, but meaning is evidently closely connected with information. What, then, is the relation between information and the meaning of sentences? I cannot provide a complete answer to this question, nor can anyone that I know of. If the propositional analysis of information is correct, a complete explication of the relation between meaning and information would require that a complete account be provided of what meaning is, what propositions are, and how meaning determines the propositions expressed by sentences. It is safe to say that the problems involved in such a task are among the most important and difficult of perennial philosophical problems, and that I am hardly able to solve them in the course of this investigation.

The precise nature of the connection between information and meaning is still not understood, but on the other hand, this problem is not a new philosophical puzzle. Given the propositional analysis of information, it really amounts to the problem of the precise nature of the connection between meaning and propositions, a traditional philosophical problem. Thus we may expect that as progress is made on this latter problem, it will translate easily into progress on the former problem as well.

Despite the fact that I am unable to present the whole story about the connection between information (or propositions) and meaning, there are still one or two points that must be made regarding this topic for later use. To begin with, I view meaning as the crucial mediating factor between sentences and propositions by virtue of which the former are able to express the latter. A sentence is a string of symbols meeting certain conditions of grammaticality, and by itself it does not express any claim about the way the world is. A proposition, on the other hand, is a language independent representation of the way the world is, with no essential connection to sentences whatever. Meaning is the bridge that connects sentences with propositions, enabling the former to express the latter. However, as we have already noted many times, a given sentence may express many different propositions, depending on various contextual factors. Thus the meaning of a sentence picks out a proposition in concert with *context*.

We may formalize the specification of contexts by agreeing to describe contexts by means of indices, where an *index* is an ordered tuple of *co-ordinates* fixing the various features of a context. What co-ordinates must be included in an index? Among other things,

> we must have a *time coordinate*, in view of tensed sentences and such sentences as 'Today is Tuesday'; a *place coordinate*, in view of such sentences as 'Here there are tigers'; a *speaker coordinate*, in view of such sentences as 'I am Porky'; an *audience coordinate*, in view of such sentences as 'You are Porky'; an *indicated objects coordinate*, in view of such sentences as 'That pig is Porky' or 'Those men are Communists'; and a *previous discourse coordinate*, in view of such sentences as 'The aforementioned pig is Porky' (Lewis 1972, 175).

Other co-ordinates are required as well, but further discussion of the exact constitution of indices would lead us too far from our topic. The important point is that we may take contexts to be formally specifiable by indices, which are ordered tuples of some sort, whose co-ordinates in turn are precisely specifiable.

Given a formal means of specifying contexts, we may now formally define sentence meaning to be *a function that maps sen-*

tences and indices into propositions.[†] For example, consider the sentence

I like ice cream.

The meaning function maps the sentence, given an index $i = \langle t, p, s, \ldots, z \rangle$ into a proposition to the effect that the speaker s likes ice cream at time t, place p, and so on. Thus it is by virtue of meaning that sentences are able to express propositions at all, and furthermore, the propositions expressed by sentences are functionally determined by meaning.

Given the propositional analysis of information, the consequence of all this is that the information carried by a sentence, or a set of sentences, is *determined* by meaning, and hence *relative* to meaning. This explains why meaning is so important for information science and especially for its application. Without an adequate theory of meaning, we lack the means to determine accurately *what* information is carried by a given sentence or set of sentences. Although rarely recognized as such, the problem of meaning is thus one of the central obstacles to progress in information science.

4.2 ELABORATION OF THE PROPOSITIONAL ANALYSIS

So far, in this chapter, we have considered the main features of the propositional analysis of information and the ontological arguments in its favor. But many questions remain regarding the nature of information. The rest of this chapter deals with a few of these questions, and explains why consideration of the others has been deferred to Chapter 9. Specifically, the subsections below examine in greater detail the various ways information is associated with sentences. The final section of this chapter lists the questions whose consideration is deferred until later and explains why they must wait.

At this point, our formal statement of the propositional analysis of information is as follows:

---

† This construal of meaning is based on Stalnaker's (1972) and Kaplan's (1979) discussions.

> The *information* carried by a set $ of sentences is the proposition
> p, where p is the conglomerate proposition expressed by a set $'
> of sentences appropriately associated with $.

This statement clearly leaves much to be desired, especially with respect to the extremely vague expression "the conglomerate proposition expressed by a set $' of sentences appropriately associated with $." It is the purpose of this section to make this characterization clear by specifying in detail what sort of relationships are the "appropriate" ones mentioned in this analysis.

The vagueness in this statement of the propositional analysis is not, of course, gratuitous; it is necessitated by the fact that the information contained in some sentences may, in some cases, differ from the information transferred by those sentences to a given individual, which may in turn differ from the information conveyed by those sentences to that individual. (The reader is reminded that the senses of 'contain', 'transfer', and 'convey' operative throughout this discussion are those delineated in section 1.1.3.) Consequently, *which* conglomerate proposition expressed by a set of sentences is the one "appropriately associated" with the sentence in question may differ depending on whether one is interested in the information contained, transferred, or conveyed. Hence, making the propositional analysis more precise requires that we consider separately the cases of the information contained in, transferred by, and conveyed by a set of sentences.

4.2.1 Information Contained

Recall that the information contained in a sentence was characterized as the information associated with the sentence by virtue of its having truth conditions. There are two points that must be considered in blending this characterization with the propositional analysis. First, a sentence's truth conditions are not fixed, since the proposition expressed by a sentence varies with the occasion of its use. Second, we need to account for the information contained in *sets* of sentences, not just single sentences. We consider these points in turn.

A sentence's truth conditions depend on the proposition the sentence expresses, but which proposition a sentence expresses depends on the context of its use, in concert with the meaning of the sentence. Thus we cannot usually say, regarding some sentence, that it absolutely contains some piece of information. Rather, we must acknowledge in our analysis that the information contained in a sentence is a function of contextual factors, as determined by the meaning of the sentence. As noted above, it is not the business of this study to consider the details of the way meaning determines the information contained in a sentence according to context. In other words, although we won't worry about *how* meaning determines information on the basis of context, we must make provision for the fact *that* it does so.

I propose to account for the role of meaning in determining information on the basis of context by making use of the formalization (presented in the last section), of meaning as a function that maps sentences and indices to propositions. Consequently, we do not hereafter refer to the information contained in a sentence S *simpliciter*, but to the information contained in S *in context i* (where i is an index specifying a context, as above). This feature is incorporated into the analysis of the notion of containing information formulated below.

The second point that must be considered in formulating an analysis of the notion of containing information in accord with the propositional analysis of information is that this notion must be broadened to account for the information contained in a set of sentences rather than just a single sentence. This really presents no difficulty, in light of our discussion above (in section 4.1.3), of the way a set of sentences may jointly carry a single piece of information. In that discussion, the propositional analysis, which was initially stated in terms of single sentences, was extended to sets of sentences by way of the device of the conglomerate proposition. We avail ourselves of the same strategy here. In particular, we make the following definition:

Let $\$ = \{S_1, S_2, \ldots, S_n\}$ be a set of sentences in a language L, f the meaning function for L, and i an index. Let $p_1, p_2, \ldots, p_n$ be the propositions expressed by the sentences $S_1, S_2, \ldots, S_n$ in context i, respectively. (That is, let $p_k = f(S_k, i)$, for all $1 < = k < = n$). Then the *conglomerate proposition expressed by the sentences of $ in context i* is the proposition formed by conjoining the propositions $p_1, p_2, \ldots, p_n$.

Note that this definition incorporates the conclusion that the analysis must be relativized to contexts.

We are now in a position to state and illustrate the propositional analysis of the notion of the information contained in a set of sentences:

> The *information contained* in a set $ of sentences in context i is the proposition p where p is the conglomerate proposition expressed by $ in context i.

To illustrate this analysis, we may consider a passage of text:

> APL was designed to extend mathematical notation, and thus to encourage symbolic thinking. For example, when thinking about multiplying two conformable matrices, does one naturally think in terms of loops, indexing over rows and columns, and storage of intermediate results? No, or at least one ought not need to involve oneself in such tedious bookkeeping details (Bettinger 1981).

This passage is a good illustration because it exhibits the extremes in complexity of determining what information is contained in a given set of sentences on the basis of contextual factors. The first sentence simply contains the information that APL was designed to extend mathematical notation and that this extension serves to encourage symbolic thinking. The second sentence is a question, and contains no information. However, the third sentence begins by answering the question in the negative, which, given the rules of English, means that this last sentence (in this context), contains the information that people do not naturally think in terms of loops, indexing over rows and columns, and the storage of intermediate results, when thinking about multiplying two conformable matrices, or at least that people ought not need to think about these things. Thus, as a whole, the passage contains information about APL, and about what people naturally think about, or what they ought not need to think about, when thinking about multiplying conformable matrices. The difficulty in determining all this, of course, arises from the subtle and complex ways that we can use our language to express propositions.

4.2.2 Information Transferred

We can employ the new analysis of the information contained in a set of sentences in analyzing the notion of the information transferred by a set of sentences. The major new factor present in cases of transferring information is that the sentences must be received (i.e., heard or read) and understood—in short, it is necessary to specify in our analysis that there be a *receiver* of the information contained in the sentences.

It is not enough, however, that there simply be a receiver of information; we must relativize the information transferred to individuals. This requirement arises from the fact that the same set of sentences, used on a given occasion, may transfer different information to different individuals. Ample illustration of this phenomena is present in every lecture or public address, or in the reading of any substantial body of text by different individuals. Through all sorts of lapses of attention while reading and listening, through unfamiliarity with vocabulary, and through difficulties in making out what is being said or has been written, people typically fail to receive or understand a few sentences here and there in any text or talk. Furthermore, different people miss different sentences. Hence despite having been exposed to the same sentences, different information is transferred by these sentences to different people. Therefore the particular person to whom information has been transferred is of crucial importance in determining precisely what information has been transferred.

Once a set of sentences has been isolated as those which *have* been received and understood by a given individual in a particular context, then the information transferred is simply the information contained in these sentences. Thus we may analyze the notion of the information transferred to a particular individual as follows:

Let $ be a set of sentences. The *information* (if any) *transferred* to Y by a set $ of sentences in context i is the proposition p if
1. $ is presented to Y in context i,
2. $' is the subset of $ consisting of only those sentences in $ heard and understood by Y,
3. p is the conglomerate proposition expressed by $' in context i.

It goes without saying that no information is transferred if $'$ is empty; one may speak in English for hours to someone who speaks only Russian and transfer no information.

An obvious, though important consequence of our analysis of the information contained in a set of sentences and the information transferred by a set of sentences is that the latter is always part of the former; the information transferred to an individual by a set of sentences is that part of the information contained in the sentences that manages to be communicated to that individual. There is, then, a systematic and rather close connection between the information contained in sentences and the information transferred by them.

4.2.3 Information Conveyed

We have established that there is a strong systematic relationship between the information contained in sentences and the information transferred by them. As we will see, this sort of relationship does not extend to the information conveyed by sentences. The factor that blocks any strong systematic connection between the information contained or transferred, and the information conveyed, is that the information, if any, conveyed to some individual is in part dependent upon the previous beliefs of that individual and on what that individual comes to believe as a result of receiving and understanding a message. For, as discussed in Chapter 1, the information conveyed by sentences is associated with the change in belief-state, if any, of the recipient of the sentences. The introduction of belief into our considerations complicates matters quite a bit, and will exercise us considerably in this section.

The first condition that apparently needs to be satisfied in order for a set of sentences $ to convey information to an individual Y is that Y must receive and understand some sentences of $. For example, it hardly seems plausible that Newton's *Principia*, which I have never read, has conveyed any information to me. Furthermore, even if someone were to read me the original, it still doesn't seem that any information would be conveyed to me, since I don't understand Latin. On the other hand, it does seem that Kant's first *Critique* has conveyed some information to me, even though I have read only about the first third of it, and understand only a fraction of that. Thus it seems that in order to convey information to an individual, at least part of a set of sentences must be received and understood by the individual, but this may be a proper part of the whole. There doesn't seem to be any magical fraction of a set of sentences that must be read and understood in order that it be appropriate to say that the sentences in the set have conveyed information, so we might as well settle on the following: at least one sentence in a set of sentences $ must be received and understood by an individual Y in order for the sentences of $ to convey information to Y.

The last conclusion allows us to establish that there is a weak relationship between transferring and conveying information. All that is required in order that a set $ of sentences transfer information to an individual Y is that Y receive and understand some sentence of $. Thus we may conclude that information is conveyed to Y by the sentences of $ only if information is transferred to Y by the sentences of $. Therefore a necessary condition of a set of sentences' conveying information to Y is that the set of sentences transfer information to Y (and hence that $ also contain information).

On the other hand, neither the fact that a set of sentences contains information, nor the fact that it is used to transfer information to Y on some occasion, are sufficient conditions for its being the case that the sentences in the set convey information to Y on that occasion. It is obvious that containing information is not sufficient for conveying information, for a set of sentences may contain information but never be read by the individual Y and so never convey information to Y.

It is less obvious that transferring information is not sufficient for conveying information. To make our case, it is necessary to bring into play the fact that information is conveyed to an individual only if that individual's belief-state is altered. As stressed above, the transfer of information to an individual does not depend at all upon whether the individual's beliefs are altered. Thus an individual may read and understand a sentence which contains information, and thereby have information transferred to him or her, without altering his or her beliefs in the slightest, and hence without having any information conveyed to him or her. This argument can be made more concrete by illustrating it with an example. Suppose my car is dented in a minor accident, and that a few days later (by which time I believe both that my car has been dented and that all of my friends know that this is the case) my friend X tells me that, in case it had somehow escaped my attention, my car was dented. Now supposing that I do not bother to draw some obvious conclusions (I do not come to believe, for example, that not all my friends knew I knew my car was dented), this is a case where my belief-state is unchanged by the message that my car was dented. I suggest that this is likewise a case in which one's intuition is that, indeed, no information is conveyed to me by this message. Yet information is transferred to me: I receive and understand a message that the world is a certain way. Hence we may conclude, in light of this counter-example, that transferring information to an individual does not guarantee that any information has been conveyed to that individual.

We have now managed to establish one necessary condition of conveying information, and to substantiate the claim that the information conveyed by a set of sentences is not very strongly related to the information contained in, or transferred by, the set of sentences. We now turn to a more thorough consideration of the connection between conveying information and changing beliefs.

To begin with, not every change in belief-state is associated with the conveyance of information. Armchair speculation about the world often leads to changes in belief unprompted by the reception of any messages whatever, so such changes in an individual's beliefs are clearly unrelated to the phenomenon of conveying information. The sort of change in belief relevant here must be one caused by messages. But again, not every sort of change in belief-state caused by a message can plausibly be regarded as being part of the information conveyed by the message. For example, suppose that Smith says "Gold has been down all month" to Jones, and Jones comes to believe that Smith has a cold because she sounds hoarse. Is it plausible to maintain that the sentence 'Gold has been down all month' *conveys* to Jones the information that Smith has a cold? It seems not. Any sentence uttered by Smith to Jones would have done as well to cause Jones to come to believe that Smith has a cold, but not every sentence uttered in that situation should convey the same information. The change in belief reflecting the information conveyed by sentences must be caused by the sentences *by virtue of what they mean,* and not by virtue of accidental features of the occasion of their use. It must therefore be the case that the change in an individual's belief-state reflecting the information conveyed by a set of sentences must be caused by the sentences in the set by virtue of the information transferred by them to the individual.

Not even every change in an individual's belief-state caused by sentences by virtue of the information they transfer to the individual reflects information conveyed to the individual by the sentences. Consider the following counter-example: suppose that Jones is a generally rational individual who believes that there are not psychic phenomena, but that one day Jones has a strong premonition and suddenly comes to believe (unaccountably, as it were) that his life is in danger. Suppose further that Jones mentions this odd experience to his friend Smith. Smith proceeds to reason with Jones about the irrationality of his belief that his life is in danger. Jones agrees with everything Smith says, of course, since Jones has always believed that reports of psychic phenomena are hogwash anyway. In other words, Smith doesn't really tell Jones anything that Jones doesn't believe already; Smith really only reminds Jones of what he believes. At Smith's urging, and in the clear light of reason, Jones soon relinquishes his belief that his life is in danger, although none of his other beliefs are changed.

The important features of this example are as follows: Smith delivers a lecture to Jones who hears and understands him, and who, by virtue of what Smith says, changes his beliefs. Smith thus transfers information to Jones. Yet nothing that Smith says to Jones is "news to Jones"—Jones believes everything that Smith says already. And the only change in Jones' beliefs is the dismissal of a belief that wasn't particularly consistent with Jones' other beliefs. Has Smith conveyed information to Jones? It seems that Smith clearly has not. Nothing that Smith says causes Jones to learn anything about the world; certainly Jones would not say that Smith's talk has been at all "informative." Hence it appears that not every change in belief-state occasioned by the transfer of information is one in which information is conveyed.

I suggest that the final requirement that must be satisfied in order for a change in belief-state to qualify as one associated with the conveyance of information is that there must be at least one proposition that the individual in question *comes to believe*. A change in belief-state (like the one above) in which a belief is relinquished but no belief adopted does not qualify as a change that reflects any conveyed information. For example, suppose that Jones had not only relinquished his belief that his life was in danger, but was so convinced by Smith's diatribe that he came to believe that his life was, on the contrary, quite safe. Then Jones would have come to believe that his life was safe by virtue of Smith's talk, so Smith would have conveyed to Jones the information that his life was safe.

We may summarize the findings of the last few pages as follows: a change in Y's belief-state is associated with information conveyed to Y by a set of sentences $ only if Y comes to believe at least one proposition by virtue of information transferred to Y by the sentences of $. What this amounts to is a statement of the conditions governing whether a set of sentences conveys information to an individual; but the question of what this information *is* remains to be answered.

The answer to this question in terms of the propositional analysis is probably already obvious to the reader. If p is the proposition that Y has come to believe by virtue of information transferred to Y by the sentences in the set $, then clearly p is the information conveyed to Y by $. We may illustrate this account by considering a simple example. Suppose that Jones attends a lecture about the Voyager mission to Saturn and, as a result of what he hears, comes to believe several things that he did not believe before. Specifically, suppose Jones learns that the Casini division contains rings, that the F-ring has two shepherd moons, and that the rings exhibit spokes, blotches, and braids. What Jones comes to believe is the proposition p that the Casini division contains rings, and the F-ring has two shepherd moons, and the rings exhibit spokes, blotches, and braids. Now consider the information conveyed to Jones; it is the information that the Casini division contains rings, and the F-ring has two shepherd moons, and the rings exhibit spokes, blotches, and braids. In short, the information conveyed to Jones by the lecture is the information that P. Formally, then, our analysis of the information conveyed is as follows:

The *information* (if any) *conveyed* to Y by the set $ of sentences in context i is the proposition p if
1. there exists information q transferred to Y by $ in context i,
2. Y comes to believe that p by virtue of the information q.

There should be no surprise at seeing the reference to context pop up in this explication, for as discussed above, context is important in determining what information is transferred, and since the transfer of at least some information is required in the analysis, the context must be included as well.

The reader at this point may be left with some nagging doubts about the propositional analysis on account of the gap between transferring information and conveying information. How is communication possible without a tighter connection between transferring information and conveying information, especially since there is so close a relationship between containing and transferring information? Communication is possible, though not foolproof, because *usually* transferring the information that P is sufficient for conveying the information that P, though, as we have seen, this is not *necessarily* the case. Typically, when X wishes to get Y to come to believe that P (i.e., X wishes to convey the information that P to Y), X frames a sentence containing the information that P, and sends it (i.e., says it or writes it down and sends the text) to Y, thereby (if all goes well) transferring the information that P to Y. Then, if Y is convinced of the veracity of X's claim, Y comes to believe that P and the communication is completed.

But as we all know, much can go awry in this sequence of events. First, X may fail to produce a text containing the information that P. Even if a suitable text is produced, it may not be successfully transferred to Y, for X may fail to send the message, or it may fail to go where it is supposed to go, or Y may not understand the text that he or she receives. Finally, even if successfully transferred, the information may not be conveyed to Y because Y might not come to believe that P, or Y may already believe that P. It is easy enough to come up with many examples illustrating all these eventualities in everyday experience.

Thus the rather loose connection between the information transferred and the information conveyed by sentences does not rule out the phenomenon of communication, but indeed corresponds to the everyday facts regarding the common difficulties of communication.

4.3 FURTHER QUESTIONS

The reader will no doubt have noticed that at least two substantial problems concerning the nature of information have been completely ignored in this chapter, namely the problem, on the one hand, of whether a proposition must be true to be information, and on the other, whether a proposition must come to be believed by some individual to be information. The former problem is completely unaddressed, but a particular position regarding the latter is presumed in the discussions of information contained, transferred, and conveyed.

Other, less important questions have likewise so far been unaddressed. No attention has been paid to whether any conditions are required of the "originator" of information contained in, transferred by, or conveyed by sentences. For example, we have not considered whether someone must believe that P in order to transfer or convey to another the information that P, or whether the "informant" must be generally reliable, or be in a position to know that P.

Many issues, then, remain to be considered in our investigation of the nature of information. They are all deferred, however, until we have carried out an investigation of informing and misinforming. The reason for this delay is simply that once a complete analysis of informing is available, it will be possible to extend many of the conclusions about informing to conclusions about information, thus easily providing solutions to many of the problems listed above. The discussion of informing and misinforming carried out in the next four chapters, then, is not only an investigation of the ordinary language notions of informing and misinforming; it is also the foundation for the last portion of our discussion of the nature of information, which occurs in Chapter 9.

5
BASIC CONSTRAINTS ON INFORMING AND MISINFORMING

The present chapter begins an investigation, pursued through the next three chapters, of the ordinary notions of informing and misinforming. The immediate goal of this part of our investigation is to provide an adequate analysis of these notions; the mediate goal is that of formulating conclusions about these notions that may be extended into corresponding conclusions regarding information and misinformation.

In outline, the discussion carried out in these four chapters consists of the following: the current chapter is devoted to establishing one of the more obvious, but still important, features of informing and misinforming, namely that X informs (or misinforms) Y that P only if Y receives and understands a message expressing the proposition that P. Chapter 6 takes up the more important issue (particularly when it comes to distinguishing informing and misinforming) of the connection between informing, misinforming, and truth. In Chapter 7, questions concerning the relation between informing and believing are examined. The discussion of informing and misinforming is completed in Chapter 8 with a consideration of possible further conditions governing informing beyond those established in the preceding chapters. One of the more novel conclusions of this study, namely that an informant must be in a position to know that P in order to inform anyone that P, is defended in this chapter. Chapter 8 culminates in presentations of analyses of 'inform' and 'misinform' based on the findings of Chapters 5 through 8.

Throughout the discussion of informing and misinforming, attention is generally focused on the former, and the latter is hardly mentioned. This is done in an effort to save both space and time, under the assumption that, except with regard to their relationships to truth, informing and misinforming share all essential features. The reader, if disinclined to make this assumption, will find that virtually all of the claims and arguments made about 'inform' in the next few chapters translate into equivalent claims and arguments about 'misinform' by substituting the latter term for the former and perhaps slightly changing a few examples.

The case that Y must receive and understand a message expressing the proposition that P in order that X inform Y that P is made as follows. First, I examine the difference between saying and telling and then determine whether informing is a kind of saying or a kind of telling. The results of these considerations, combined with some further evidence provided by paradigmatic cases of informing, establish the desired result.

5.1 SAYING AND TELLING

For ease of discussion, in this section the argument proceeds by considering only verbal communication, under the assumption that conclusions about verbal communication readily convert into conclusions about written communication, at least as concerns saying and telling.

Let us begin by examining the thesis that telling entails saying, that is, that X tells Y that P only if X says to Y that P. An immediate objection to this thesis arises in the form of purported counterexamples to it, consisting of all those cases that fall under the rubric of "telling without coming right out and saying." For example, suppose that Jones teaches mathematics and is telling his class about an upcoming test. Jones' official policy is not to reveal the specific topics covered in his tests. Suppose that in answer to a question about whether students will be expected to know how to integrate trigonometric functions, Jones replies: "I can't say, but I would strongly recommend that you all know how to integrate trigonometric functions before you take the test." One naturally describes this as being a situation in which Jones *tells* his students one of the specific topics of the test without coming right out and *saying* it. Or, at least one would describe the situation in this way if Jones typically said this sort of thing as a means of backsliding on his policy of not indicating the specific topics of tests; if Jones gave this sort of answer to *any* question about what would be on the test, then his statement couldn't be taken as telling the students anything. In other words, if Jones and his students had come to operate under the convention that when Jones "strongly recommends" that they know something, then that item would probably be on the test, we would say that Jones was really telling his students what would be on the test without explicitly saying so. The objection, then, is that telling does not entail saying, because, as this example illustrates, it is possible to tell someone that P without coming right out and saying that P.

In reply, I suggest that in situations like the one in the example, saying really is taking place, and that it is only this that makes the telling possible. Specifically, I claim that Jones really *does* say that integrating trigonometric functions will be on the test. It is true that Jones' utterance does not normally express this proposition. But given the conventions that we must presume to be in effect for it to be the case that Jones tells his class what is on the test, given these conventions, Jones' utterance does express a claim about what will be on the test.

The reply can perhaps be made clearer and more convincing by appealing to the distinction (discussed in section 1.1.3) between what a speaker's *words* mean and what a *speaker* means in using certain words, on some occasion. In this example, Jones' *words* do not mean that integrating trigonometric functions will be on the test; Jones does not *literally* say (i.e., "come right out and say") that this topic is covered on the test. However, given the conventions governing the exchange, it is clear that Jones meant, and *in effect* said, that integrating trigonometric functions would be on the test.

Thus the purported counter-example still employs saying, albeit not literally saying, that P in the course of telling the students that P. Examples like the one above therefore fail to show that telling does not entail saying.

It might be further objected that there are still counter-examples in which telling occurs without saying even in a broad sense. For example, suppose Smith and Jones are discussing the merits of a novel that they have both read, and Smith is quite consistent in praising many facets of the book, although Smith never comes right out and says that the novel is a very good novel. On the basis of this conversation, Jones concludes that Smith thinks that the book is very good. Then, it may be claimed, Smith has told Jones that he believes the book to be very good despite having not said, even in a broad sense, that this was so.

To this objection I reply that Smith has not, *except metaphorically*, told Jones that Smith believes the novel to be very good. In metaphorical terms, shoes, rocks, bottles, and buildings, in fact virtually any sort of thing, can "tell" us that something is the case. For example, the mud on my shoes may "tell" you that I have been walking in the park. But, literally speaking, my shoes (and other such items) don't talk, and they don't really tell anyone anything. Rather, we are able to draw conclusions about the way the world is based on the characteristics or behavior of things like shoes, rocks, bottles, buildings, and people. This includes many instances of drawing conclusions based on what people say and how they say it. Thus, in considering what can be learned from what has been said, care must be taken to distinguish genuine cases of telling from cases of drawing conclusions which are only metaphorically cases of telling.

Returning to the alleged counter-example, I reiterate that it exhibits at best only a case of metaphorical telling. Smith does not literally tell Jones that he likes the book; rather Jones comes to this conclusion on the basis of Smith's statements that he likes certain aspects of the book. This may be brought out by noting that if Smith were to state that he did not think that the novel was a good one, Jones could not justifiably accuse Smith of telling any lies about how he felt about the book. For Smith could very well like many aspects of the book without believing it to be, on balance, a good novel. Rather, Jones must be counted as having made an inference on the basis of what Smith said which may turn out to be incorrect. The counter-example fails, then, because it does not exhibit a genuine case of telling, and so does not present an instance of telling without saying.

The thesis that telling entails saying seems to stand up to objections. We may now ask whether the converse holds as well, that is, whether saying entails telling.

It is easy to generate examples showing that saying does not entail telling. These counter-examples may be divided into two groups, each group illustrating a way that saying may occur without telling. The first group of counter-examples shows that X may say to Y that P without succeeding in telling Y that P because Y fails to *hear* X say that P. Examples of this sort are frequent (unfortunately) in everyday life, as the familiarity of the following dialogue shows:

Smith: Why didn't you meet me for lunch?
Jones: I didn't know that I was supposed to.
Smith: But I told you last night!
Jones: I'm sure you didn't.
Smith: *I'm sure* that I said that you should meet me for lunch.
Jones: Then I guess I didn't hear you.

Smith first insists that she told Jones to meet her, then weakens her position to an insistence that at least she said that Jones should meet her. Jones denies having been told to meet Smith and explains this as a failure to hear the message. Smith said that P, but Jones didn't hear her, so Smith failed to tell Jones that P. Thus saying to someone that P is *part* of what is involved in telling them that P, but only a part—it must also be the case that the person to whom it is said that P hears what is said.

The second group of counter-examples shows that not even hearing what is said is enough to guarantee that in saying to someone that P, one tells them that P. Suppose that Jones speaks only Russian and Smith speaks only English, and that Smith tries to tell Jones that Mars has two moons by saying to Jones "Mars has two moons." Although Jones hears what Smith says perfectly, Jones is not told that Mars has two moons because Jones does not understand a word of what Smith says. Thus *understanding* what is said, as well as hearing what is said, is required of the person being told if telling is indeed to take place.

Are there any further conditions required to guarantee that when X says to Y that P, then X tells Y that P? None of the obvious candidates for this role seem to be required. Certainly it is not required that P be true for X to succeed in telling Y that P; as everyone knows, people tell one another falsehoods frequently. Furthermore, neither belief on the part of the teller nor on the part of the person being told seems to be required for telling to take place. Regarding the former, one need only note that lack of belief on the part of the speaker in what he or she says is an essential feature of that sort of telling called "lying." Hence one may tell another that P without believing that P. Likewise, regarding the latter, it is common for someone to disbelieve what he or she is told, so telling someone that P does not hinge on their believing, or coming to believe, that P.

The intentions of the speaker also seem to be irrelevant for successful telling; in particular, it is not required that X *intend* to tell Y that P for X to succeed in telling Y that P. For X may inadvertently tell Y that P; things often just "slip out," as we say, without our really intending them to.

I conclude, then, that no further conditions beyond the requirement that what is said be heard and understood are needed to insure that in saying to Y that P, X also tells Y that P. Hence,

> X *tells* Y that P if X says to Y that P and Y hears and understands what X says, namely, that P.

This biconditional expresses the relationship between telling and saying quite perspicuously, but of course it leaves out any characterization of what "saying that P" consists in. In concluding this section, I discuss the notion of saying that P in terms of producing a sentence expressing the proposition that P.

The notion of 'saying that P' is framed in terms of propositions (i.e., 'that P' names a proposition, as discussed in sections 4.1.2 and 4.1.3). But, of course, what happens when someone says that P is not the occurrence of a proposition (which doesn't even make sense), but the occurrence of an utterance, the verbal production of one or more sentence tokens. To say that P, one must utter tokens of one or more sentences which, given the meaning of the sentences and the context of use, express the proposition that P. *Which* sentences one uses to say that P are irrelevant, as long as the utterance does result in the assertion that P. For example, one can say that it is four-fifteen by uttering the sentence 'It is four-fifteen' or the sentence 'It is a quarter past four'. Thus, saying that P involves uttering sentence tokens which, given the context of utterance, express the proposition that P.

In light of this fact, broadening our scope to include written as well as verbal communication, and employing one of the technical devices developed in Chapter 4, we may analyze telling as follows:

X *tells* Y that P if there exists a set $ of sentences such that
1. X sends $ to Y in context i,
2. Y receives and understands the sentences of $,
3. p is the conglomerate proposition expressed by $ in context i.

It should be noted that this analysis does not require that Y understand *everything* that X may say to Y. The set $ may be a subset of the set of sentences that X says to Y, namely the subset of sentences that X says to Y that Y hears and understands.

5.2 TELLING AND INFORMING

The question to be settled in this section is "Does informing someone that P require that the person informed receive and understand a message expressing the proposition that P?" In light of the discussion in the last section, this question may be rephrased in terms of saying and telling as "Is informing a kind of telling or is it merely a kind of saying?" One's immediate inclination (or at least my immediate inclination) is to say that, whatever informing is, it is at least as strong as telling—when X informs Y that P, X has at least told Y that P. On this basis, it seems clear that informing does require receiving and understanding a message. However, to make sure of this conclusion, I consider some paradigm cases of informing to see whether it is borne out.

One of the best examples of informing occurs when people in this country are arrested. For when someone is arrested, the police are required to inform that person of his or her rights under the law. In informing someone of his or her rights, the arresting officer must not only *say* to the individual that he or she has certain rights, the officer must also make sure that that individual *understands* his or her rights as the officer has given them. Thus if the person being arrested does not understand English, an interpreter must be found to tell that person his or her rights before there can be any questioning. Thus informing someone that P requires that an individual understand that P, at least in the eyes of the law.

Another good example of informing is what goes on in the news media. For example, we say that Dan Rather informs his viewers that such and such has occurred. Let us consider the details of this sort of activity. Suppose that a technical problem causes Rather's voice to vanish from the television set just as he is saying, for example, that the Pope has undergone another operation. Rather does say that the Pope has undergone another operation, though his viewers cannot hear him. In this situation it seems clear that Rather does not inform his viewers about the Pope. Hence hearing or reading the message that P is required for being informed that P.

Now suppose that the situation is as follows: Rather says "The Pope has undergone another operation," and this sentence is clearly heard by a viewer who watches the news even though he cannot understand English. Has Rather informed this viewer that the Pope has undergone another operation? Obviously not. Hence understanding is likewise required for informing.

5.3 CONCLUSION

In light of these considerations, it seems safe to conclude that informing is a species of telling. Hence

X *informs* Y that P only if X tells Y that P.

Given the analysis of 'tell' stated above, we may expand this statement of the conclusion as follows:

X *informs* Y that P only if there exists a set $ of sentences such that
    1. X sends $ to Y in context i,

2. Y receives and understands the sentences of $,
3. p is the conglomerate proposition expressed by $ in context
   i.

This necessary condition of informing of course extends to misinforming as well; misinforming is also a kind of telling.

Having determined that saying and telling are basic constraints on informing and misinforming, we turn in the next chapter to a much more difficult problem, namely the relationship between informing, misinforming, and truth. The conclusion of this chapter will eventually figure in the analyses of 'inform' and 'misinform' presented in Chapter 8.

6
INFORMING, MISINFORMING, AND TRUTH

The difference between informing and misinforming seems to hinge on, or ultimately depend on, the fact that sometimes what one person tells another is true and sometimes it is false. Indeed, one is inclined to divide all cases in which X tells Y that P into two mutually exclusive and exhaustive classes on the basis of whether p is true or false. Then the class of cases where p is true contains all the instances in which X informs Y that P, while the class of cases where p is false contains all the instances in which X misinforms Y that P.

This account is very simple and tidy, and furthermore it appears to accord with the facts concerning the ordinary use of the terms 'inform' and 'misinform'. This appearance, however, vanishes when we consider various examples a little more closely.

For example, suppose that Jones is an inventor who dreams up a new gizmo for sharpening razor blades. Jones thinks that he can make a fortune if he can produce and distribute his invention, but he needs capital to set up his operation. Consequently, Jones arranges a meeting with a group of investors and informs them that (among other things) his product has been successfully tested by a group of consumers. Now in fact this is hogwash—Jones is merely saying whatever he can think of to persuade people to invest in his invention. Nonetheless, it seems correct to say that Jones has *informed* these people that his product has been fully tested. And if Jones is brought to court for fraud, it would be because he informed the investors that his product was tested when in fact this was not the case.

I do not suggest that this example (or others like it) provides enough evidence to conclude that informing does not require truth. Nevertheless, this example does cast doubt on the simple account of the relation between informing, misinforming, and truth suggested in the first two paragraphs above. For if that account is correct, it should not be possible to say (correctly) that Jones informed his investors that his gizmo was fully tested; it should be necessary to describe the situation as one in which Jones misinforms his investors that his invention was fully tested. Thus we have reason to be suspicious of the adequacy of the simple account above, and motivation to look more deeply into the connection between informing, misinforming, and truth.

The present chapter takes up this inquiry. The goal of the discussion is to determine whether informing requires truth and whether misinforming requires falsity. Put more formally and precisely, we will seek to answer the following questions:

1. Do sentences of the form "X informs Y that P" entail P?
2. Do sentences of the form "X misinforms Y that P" entail not-P?

(It should be understood that X and Y stand for expressions denoting individuals, and P stands for an indicative sentence.) These questions are questions about whether the entailment relation holds between sentences of a certain form. Furthermore, the sentences in question bear a certain syntactic relation to one another: the sentence S is the complement sentence of both the sentence 'X informs Y that S' and 'X misinforms Y that S'. Finally, in both cases, whether the entailment obtains or not depends on the peculiar features of the words 'inform' and 'misinform'. Consequently, questions 1 and 2 are specific instances of more general questions regarding entailment relations holding between certain sentences and their complement sentences by virtue of the logical features of a certain class of terms (among which are 'inform' and 'misinform'), called "sentence-complementing terms." In order to arrive at the firmest possible conclusion regarding 'inform' and 'misinform', we will conduct an extensive investigation into the entailments that obtain by virtue of sentence-complementing terms generally, and apply the results to the particular cases of 'inform' and 'misinform'.

In outline, then, the chapter is organized as follows: since the questions we are concerned to answer are about the entailment relation, the discussion begins with a consideration of entailment and of the criteria to be employed in deciding whether entailments obtain. Once this is done, several distinct classes of sentence-complementing terms will be distinguished on both syntactic and semantic grounds, and conclusions about the entailments, if any, arising by virtue of the terms in the various classes will be reached. Armed with these conclusions, it will then be possible to determine what sorts of sentence-complementing terms the words 'inform' and 'misinform' are, and hence to determine the answers to questions 1 and 2.

6.1 SENTENCE-COMPLEMENTING TERMS

Before undertaking a discussion of entailment, it will be worthwhile to explain more clearly what a sentence-complementing term is and to adopt some terminology for discussing such terms.

Very many sentences in English are such that they have proper parts which themselves are English sentences. For example, the sentence "It's too bad that John had to leave early" has a proper part which is a sentence, namely "John had to leave early." If a sentence S has a proper part T which itself is a sentence, then T is said to be a *complement sentence* of S. There are certain verbs and adjectives in English which (in certain uses) occur in sentences with complements. Examples of such words are 'true', 'necessary', 'regret', 'lucky', 'believe', and so on; a few illustrations using these examples are the following:

It's true that he left without a word.

John appears to regret that his actions caused such misery.

It's lucky no one saw you.

Terms which behave in this way are called *sentence-complementing terms*. Both 'inform' and 'misinform' are, as has been noted, sentence-complementing terms.

Verbs and adjectives, when viewed in the context of first-order logic, behave as predicates; in other words, they are used to ascribe properties to individuals, or relations to two or more individuals. From this perspective, we may describe sentence-complementing terms as predicates at least one of whose arguments is a sentence (i.e., the complement-sentence). Furthermore, we may employ standard terminology in distinguishing *one-place* sentence-complementing terms, *two-place* sentence-complementing terms, and so on, and in general, *n-place* sentence-complementing terms. Later on, when we distinguish several classes of sentence-complementing terms, and name these classes, we will employ this terminology with these names; hence we will refer to "one-place factives," "three-place assertives," and so forth. For example, as we will see, 'tragic' is a one-place factive since this word is a member of the class of factive sentence-complementing words, and it is a predicate whose single argument is a sentence. Similarly, 'reveal to' is a three-place assertive since it is a member of the class of assertives and it needs three arguments: two expressions designating individuals (the "revealer" and the "revealee"), and a sentence.

6.1.1 Entailment

Entailment is a relation between two sentences P and Q which can be defined as follows: P *entails* Q just in case it is impossible for P to be true and Q not to be true. (Reference to an interpretation is left out of this definition to simplify matters, since nothing of importance depends on this point.) This definition differs slightly (though significantly) from the standard definition of entailment as the relation that holds between P and Q when it is impossible for P to be true and Q to be false. The reason for this divergence will become clear later (when we discuss presupposition in section 6.1.2.2). For now, I encourage the reader to accept this definition by noting that if every sentence is either true or false, then this definition is equivalent to the standard definition.

6.1.1.1 *Two Kinds of Entailment*

We can roughly distinguish two ways in which one sentence may entail another. One way, which I call "low-level entailment," is the entailment that obtains between sentences solely by virtue of the arrangement of logical terms and operators in the sentences. For example, the sentences

A. John told me.

B. Someone told me but I didn't believe it.

both entail

C. Someone told me.

Sentence A entails C because C differs from A only in that the name 'John' has been replaced by the quantifier 'someone', and first-order logic licenses such replacements as truth-preserving. Likewise, B entails C by virtue of characteristics of the truth-functional operation of conjunction, captured in natural language by 'and', 'but', and a few other terms.

   In both cases, the entailment is preserved so long as the *logical form* of the sentences is maintained, no matter which non-logical terms are used in place of those that do occur in the sentences. Thus, for example, we may uniformly replace the words 'John', 'told', and 'believe' in the sentences above without disturbing the entailment relations that hold between the sentences:

A'. Dora hit me.

B'. Someone hit me but I didn't notice it.

C'. Someone hit me.

In this example, A' and B' both entail C', and for exactly the same reasons (respectively) as A and B entail C.

   In cases of low-level entailment like those above, the pertinent logical relations holding between sentences can be fully analyzed and explained with recourse only to first-order logic. In such analysis, the only relevant features of sentences are their truth-functional and quantificational form, without regard for the non-logical terms involved.

In contrast to low-level entailment we can distinguish another sort of entailment, which we mundanely term "high-level entailment," that *does* take aspects of non-logical terms into account. This second sort of entailment does not come about simply by virtue of the (first-order) logical form of sentences, but rather by virtue of peculiar features of certain of the non-logical terms involved. As examples, consider that the sentences

D.   It's necessary that God exists.

E.   Aquinas knows that God exists.

F.   Anselm proved that God exists.

all entail the sentence

G.   God exists.

There is no quantificational or truth-functional basis for these entailments; rather, they rely on special features of the terms 'necessary', 'knows', and 'proved', as we can easily see by considering examples in which these words have been replaced:

D'. It's possible that God exists.

E'. Aquinas believes that God exists.

F'. Anselm conjectured that God exists.

None of D', E', and F' entail G. Thus the entailments that hold between D, E, and F and conclusion G are high-level rather than low-level entailments.

We have distinguished between high- and low-level entailment, and explained how the latter depends on logical form alone while the former involves peculiar features of various non-logical terms. We may now point out that our concern throughout this chapter is with high-level entailments involving sentence-complementing words, and not with low-level entailments at all. In particular, the ultimate goal of this chapter might be stated as being the determination of whether sentences of the form 'X informs Y that P' and 'X misinforms Y that P' have any high-level entailments.

6.1.1.2 Criteria of Entailment

We have defined entailment as a relation that holds between two sentences P and Q when it is impossible for P to be true and Q not to be true. The question we consider now is "Having defined entailment, how does one go about deciding whether one sentence entails another?" In other words, given sentences P and Q, how does one decide whether it is possible for P to be true and Q false?

The basic answer to this question is that we must, when considering whether P entails Q, think carefully about it, examine various examples, consult our "logical intuitions," and when we feel convinced one way or the other, make the decision.

This answer may seem rather objectionable, and furthermore it may appear to fly in the face of the fact that very often when an entailment claim is evaluated it is formal logic, rather than logical intuitions, which are brought into play. Although true, this remark misses the point of the answer, which is that *at bottom* all judgments concerning entailment rest on logical intuitions. Systems of formal logic are not, like natural laws or continents, discovered by scientists or explorers. They are rather invented by logicians as a means of capturing and codifying important logical relations (like entailment) obtaining among sentences (or propositions). These logical relations are not *made to obtain* by formal systems, but instead are *modeled* or *mirrored* by formal systems. But a formal system designed to codify logical relations among sentences can only be built when these logical relations are recognized, and even then it is always possible to question whether a given formal system adequately captures the logical relations it is alleged to capture. The recognition of logical relations, and the assessment of the adequacy of formal systems to capture them, depends on careful thought, examination of examples, and consultation of logical intuitions. There is simply no other way to conduct such investigations.

Systems of formal logic are really formalizations of logical intuitions. When we use the tools of formal logic, we are still consulting logical intuitions, but indirectly by way of artifacts constructed to reflect the verdicts of our intuitions. It is certainly preferable to use this indirect method of consultation, since it is far more trustworthy and reliable than the direct method. However not every logical relation among sentences is captured by some presently extant formal system. Thus there are (frequent) cases in which formal logic is of no avail and intuitions regarding logical relations must be consulted directly. In particular, it will be necessary to consult directly logical intuitions regarding entailments between sentences with sentence-complementing predicates and their complement sentences. (It should be noted in passing that there is one group of sentence-complementing words for which a thorough formal logic has been developed, namely the modal predicates like 'possible', 'necessary', and so forth. Although we will consider these modal predicates, the vast majority of words with which we are concerned are not modal, and have not been investigated by logicians.)

Our basic criterion for deciding on whether an entailment obtains, then, will be carefully and thoughtfully to consult our intuitions, giving special scrutiny to all sorts of examples. This method is, of course, most reliable when we can generate a counter-example. In other words, if we can generate an example in which P is true and Q not true, then certainly P does not entail Q. Establishing that P does entail Q, however, is more difficult, because no amount of examples can guarantee that no counter-example has been overlooked. In such cases (and even when there are counter-examples), I will employ two additional tests to help sharpen intuitions and build a convincing case that an entailment obtains (or does not obtain).

The first method to test whether P entails Q is to consider statements to the effect that P and not-Q. If P really does entail Q there should be a "felt inconsistency" in asserting that P and not-Q, and otherwise not. We mark sentences that exhibit a "felt inconsistency" with the symbol '#', and consider some examples to illustrate this principle:

It's true that John left and John did not leave.

It's possible that we all passed the test, but we didn't all pass the test.

Leo conjectured that pi is rational but pi is not rational.

Leo discovered that pi is rational but pi is not rational.

John hit Mary but no one hit Mary.

John hit Mary but no one hit Lisa.

In four of these six examples, inconsistency or consistency can be proved using first order or modal logic. In all six cases, there is a felt inconsistency if our intuitions (no matter how consulted) tell us that the first conjunct entails the negation of the second.

The explanation of the efficacy of this test for entailment is quite straightforward. A conjunction is true only if both of its conjuncts are true. Hence the assertion that P and not-Q is satisfiable only if it is possible for P to be true and Q false. But of course if P entails Q then this is *not* possible, so the assertion is inconsistent and (ideally) we perceive this to be the case.

I call this first method of testing our intuitions to see whether P entails Q the *inconsistency test*, thus distinguishing it from the second method, the *consistency test*. The consistency test takes advantage of the fact that when P entails Q, the conjunction of P and Q exhibits a so-called performance oddity—although the sentence is syntactically correct, there is something odd about its assertion. Marking sentences exhibiting a performance oddity with '?', we can illustrate this fact as follows:

? It's true that John left and John left.

It's possible that we all passed the test and we did all pass the test.

Leo conjectured that pi is irrational and pi is irrational.

? Leo discovered that pi is irrational and pi is irrational.

? John knows that Florence did it and Florence did it.

John believes that Florence did it and Florence did it.

In all and only the cases where the first conjunct entails the second is a performance oddity observed.

A very good explanation of the success of the consistency test in sorting out entailments can be gotten by considering the situation in light of some work done by Grice (1975) concerning general rules and conventions governing discourse. Grice's goal is to lay the groundwork for a theory to explain how one person can communicate something to another without explicitly stating what he or she means. Grice calls such suggestions or meanings over and above what is explicitly stated *implicatures*, and he is primarily concerned with implicatures arising in everyday discourse, which he calls *conversational implicatures*. This leads Grice to an investigation of (what is really of interest for our purposes here) "certain general features of discourse." Regarding these features, Grice argues that

> our talk exchanges do not normally consist of a succession of disconnected remarks, and would not be rational if they did. They are, characteristically, to some degree at least cooperative efforts. Each participant recognizes in them, to some extent, a common purpose or set of purposes, or at least a mutually accepted direction. This purpose or direction may be fixed from the start (e.g., by an initial proposal of a question for discussion), or it may evolve during the exchange; it may be fairly definite, or it may be so indefinite as to leave very considerable latitude to the participants (as in a casual conversation). But at each stage, *some* possible conversational moves would be excluded as conversationally unsuitable. We might then formulate a rough general principle which participants will be expected (ceteris paribus) to observe, viz: "Make your conversational contribution such as is required, at the stage at which it occurs, by the accepted purpose or direction of the talk exchange in which you are engaged." One might label this the Cooperative Principle (CP) (Grice 1975, 66–67).

On the basis of this principle, Grice goes on to discuss four maxims which, he suggests, govern conversation so as to bring it in line with the Cooperation Principle.

Although Grice elaborates his discussion of the maxims with all sorts of submaxims, we can paraphrase his list in briefer fashion as follows:

1. Be as informative (but no more so) than is required for the current purposes of the exchange.
2. Be truthful.
3. Be relevant.
4. Be brief, clear, and orderly.

Justification for the claim that these maxims govern our everyday discourse is based on the assumption that there are certain goals "that are central to conversation/communication (such as giving and receiving information, influencing and being influenced by others)" (Grice 1975, 69). Given that there are such goals, it seems clear that they will be most efficiently realized (and in some cases, only realized at all) if discourse proceeds generally in accord with the Cooperation Principle and specifically in accord with the maxims. Hence we may take these conventions as governing our everyday discourse.

Grice goes on to apply these results in his larger investigation of conversational implicature, but this later discussion need not concern us now. We can, however, profitably bring Grice's maxims to bear in explaining why a performance oddity is exhibited in assertions that 'P and Q' when P entails Q. Suppose P entails Q and that P is asserted. Then it follows that Q must likewise be the case. Hence the further assertion that Q is redundant. Therefore the assertion that P and Q is less brief than it need be, for it says no more than the simple assertion that P. Therefore we can explain the performance oddity exhibited by the assertion that P and Q as accruing from the fact that such an assertion violates the conversational maxim that one be brief.

A further argument in favor of this Gricean explanation (as well as a crucial feature of the consistency text) is the following. On the Gricean view, 'P and Q' exhibits a performance oddity when P entails Q because once P is asserted it is redundant to assert Q. But note that if P and Q are not equivalent (i.e., if Q does not entail P), then the assertion that Q followed by the assertion that P is *not* redundant, and 'Q and P' should not exhibit a performance oddity. In fact, this is precisely the case: if P entails Q but not conversely, then generally 'P and Q' exhibits a performance oddity but 'Q and P' does not. We illustrate with two of the examples already considered:

? Leo discovered that pi is irrational and pi is irrational.

Pi is irrational and Leo discovered that pi is irrational.

? John knows that Florence did it and Florence did it.

Florence did it and John knows that Florence did it.

Note that in the second and fourth sentences, the 'and' has the force of 'and furthermore', and that these sentences are most comfortably read with stress on 'Leo discovered' and 'John knows', which is just what one would expect since these words provide the crucial increment of information over that provided in the respective first clauses.

In summary, then, we will employ three means of determining whether a sentence (or proposition) P entails another sentence (or proposition) Q. The first is carefully to consider examples, to consult our logical intuitions, and if P does not entail Q, to produce a counter-example. To sharpen intuitions and to reinforce whatever conclusions are arrived at, the alleged entailment (or lack thereof) is submitted to two further tests: the consistency and inconsistency tests. Ideally, the results of these investigations will allow us to determine with a high degree of confidence whether P entails Q.

6.1.2 Factives

With this section we begin to distinguish and investigate different classes of sentence-complementing terms; the first such class we consider are the factives.

The seminal and still definitive article on factives is Paul and Carol Kiparsky's "Fact" (1971). The paper begins by noting systematic differences in the syntax of sentences involving sentence-complementing terms. These differences form the basis of a syntactic division among such terms into a class of *factive* predicates and a class of *non-factive* predicates. Although relatively interesting for its own sake, the real importance of this division arises from the fact that the "syntactic differences are correlated with a semantic difference" (Kiparsky and Kiparsky 1971, 348). Specifically, the use of a factive predicate carries with it the presupposition that the embedded sentence is true. Once this correlation is established, Kiparsky and Kiparsky go on to explain the situation in terms of the deep structure of sentences containing factive predicates. They are able to account quite convincingly for the syntactic considerations that prompted their investigation, as well as the important syntactic and semantic correlation that they also note.

Although Kiparsky and Kiparsky's account of the underlying syntactic mechanisms governing factivity are important and exciting, they are quite beside the point of our present discussion. We need instead to establish (1) the syntactic criteria distinguishing factive from non-factive predicates, (2) the semantic criteria distinguishing sentences with presuppositions from those without them, and (3) the truth of the alleged connection between factivity and presupposition. To accomplish these ends, we turn to a more detailed exposition of the first portion of Kiparsky and Kiparsky's paper.

6.1.2.1 Syntactic Criteria of Factivity

Kiparsky and Kiparsky begin their exposition by listing representative factive and non-factive predicates, including those below:

Factive (One-Place)	Non-Factive (One-Place)	Factive (Two-Place)	Non-Factive (Two-Place)
significant	likely	regret	suppose
odd	sure	ignore	assert
tragic	possible	forget	allege
matters	true	resent	believe
fortunate	seems	bear in mind	conjecture
amuses	appears	make clear	assume

(Note that in many cases the order of a predicate varies—for example we may say that "S matters" or "S matters to X." Then 'matters' is a one-place predicate in the first case and a many-place predicate in the second. There are several cases in which this matters regarding whether a predicate is a factive. But to clarify matters, we simply distinguish separate predicates that are typographically indistinguishable. Thus there is the *one*-place predicate 'matters' and the different *two*-place predicate 'matters.' These distinctions can obviously be made (and indeed must be made) both syntactically and semantically.

Factives and non-factives do not differ in every construction in which they appear. Thus the surface-structure of the following pairs are identical:

It is significant that he left during the first act.

It is likely that he left during the first act.

We regret that he left during the first act.

We suppose that he left during the first act.

We quickly come to constructions in which the systematic differences between factives and non-factives arise, however. I follow Kiparsky and Kiparsky in delineating four such constructions.

(1) Constructions employing 'fact' as the head noun of the complemented sentence. If the simple *that*-clause of a well formed sentence is replaced by a construction consisting of 'the fact' followed by the simple *that*-clause or a gerund, the result is acceptable only with factive predicates. For example (I mark unacceptable sentences with the symbol *):

Factive: The fact that John hit Mary is amusing.
Non-factive: *The fact that John hit Mary is likely.
Factive: Bill regrets the fact that John hit Mary.
Non-factive: *Bill alleges the fact that John hit Mary.
Factive: The fact of his contracting hepatitis is tragic.
Non-factive: *The fact of his contracting hepatitis is possible.
Factive: I forgot the fact of his contracting hepatitis.
Non-factive: *I conjecture the fact of his contracting hepatitis.

The term 'factive' is of course derived from the fact that only factive sentence-complementing words may be used in sentences in which the head noun of the subordinate clause is the word 'fact'. There seem to be few, if any, exceptions regarding this criterion of factivity.

(2) Gerundial constructions and adjectival nominalizations in *-ness*. In constructions using factive predicates, the *that*-clause may always be replaced by all sorts of gerunds, or by an adjectival nominalization in *-ness*. This is also allowed in a few cases with non-factives, but in general it is not. Consider the following examples:

Factive: The paleness of Sue's face matters.
Non-factive: *The paleness of Sue's face is likely.
Factive: John bore in mind the paleness of Sue's face.
Non-factive: *John supposed the paleness of Sue's face.
Factive: The barking of the dog last night is important.
Non-factive: *The barking of the dog last night is true.
Factive: John minded the barking of the dog last night.
Non-factive: *John believed the barking of the dog last night.

Even more striking examples can be generated using other sorts of gerunds, as Kiparsky and Kiparsky demonstrate (Kiparsky and Kiparsky 1971, 347).

(3) Infinitive constructions. Factive predicates fail to take certain infinitive constructions that are frequently acceptable with non-factive predicates. In the case of one-place predicates, the relevant construction is to turn the initial noun-phrase of the subordinate clause into the subject of the main clause, and then convert the remaining part of the subordinate clause into an infinitive phrase. For example, this enterprise turns A into B below:

A.   It is alleged that John perpetrated the act.

B.   John is alleged to have perpetrated the act.

This sort of thing is acceptable with many (though not all) non-factives; however, it is never acceptable with factives, as the following examples suggest:

Non-factive: He is unlikely to be reappointed.
Factive: *He is odd to have perpetrated the act.
Factive: *John suffices to have perpetrated the act.

In the case of many-place predicates, the subject of the main clause is not a place holder 'it', but a noun-phrase with a substantial denotation. Hence the sort of transformation that takes place for one-place predicates is not allowed. Instead, the relevant construction is one in which the *that*-clause is replaced by an infinitive phrase. This is called the accusative and infinitive construction, and it is never allowed with factive predicates, but often with non-factive predicates:

Non-Factive: Mary believes there to have been four assailants.
              He fancies himself to be an expert in pottery.
Factive: *Mary forgot there to have been four assailants.
              *He resents himself to be an expert in pottery.

(4) Extraposition. This last criterion applies only to one-place predicates. Extraposition is the placement of a complement at the end of a sentence. Extraposition is always optional with one-place factives, but it is obligatory for several one-place non-factives. Thus consider the following examples:

Factive: That the rain has finally stopped is exciting.
               That Bacon wrote Hamlet is amusing.
Non-factive: *That the rain has finally stopped appears.
               *That Bacon wrote Hamlet turns out.

This criterion actually turns out to be not too helpful in practice because in fact quite a few non-factive predicates don't require extraposition:

Non-factive: That Bacon wrote Hamlet is possible.
              That the rain has finally stopped in Syracuse is unlikely.
              That this criterion is effective is false.

These four criteria, then, are the syntactic basis for distinguishing factive from non-factive predicates.

6.1.2.2 Semantic Criteria of Presupposition

Presupposition has been a controversial topic in philosophy for some time, although debate has focused not on presuppositions of sentences containing occurrences of various sentence-complementing terms, but on presuppositions of sentences containing definite descriptions or the ordinary language universal quantifier 'all.' In any case, misgivings about the notion of pre-supposition (which I share) are due to the fact that admitting presupposition forces the abandonment of two-valued logic in favor of three-valued logic. Besides introducing a suspect truth-value, this move also has the unfortunate consequence of losing us some of our most cherished logical principles, such as the law of excluded middle. On the other hand, the explanatory value of the notion of presupposition is very great, particularly in the case of sentence-complementing predicates. For our present purposes, the latter consideration takes precedence over the former, so we put aside philosophical qualms about presupposition in order to carry on with our investigation.

I now implicitly assume a three-valued logic adequate to deal with the notion of presupposition. For a formal and detailed account of such a "presupposition logic," see Keenan (1973).

The notion of presupposition quite naturally arises when consideration is given to the ways in which certain sentences may fail to be true. For example, consider sentence A in this regard:

A. Beauregard is sad that he didn't make the football team.

In the first place, A may fail to be true because Beauregard is actually quite pleased that he didn't make the football team—he was only trying out because his father forced him to. In this case, A fails to be true because it is false. But now suppose that in fact Beauregard *did* make the football team. Then A is definitely not true, but on the other hand, it is not quite right to say that A is false either. For this suggests that Beauregard is not sad about not making the football team, rather than that he did make the football team. Armed with the notion of presupposition, we can straighten out our difficulties as follows: sentence A *presupposes* the sentence

B. Beauregard didn't make the football team.

In order for A to be true or false, B must be true. If B is not true (i.e., the presupposition fails) then A is neither true nor false—instead it is "indeterminate," or has truth-value zero.

This example has two features especially pertinent for the remainder of our discussion. The first is that A has zero truth-value when its presupposition fails. This turns out to be the basis for a clear definition of presupposition. The second important feature of the example is that A or its negation can be true only if B is true. This indicates that *presupposition is constant under negation*. It turns out that this is the crucial fact which serves as the acid test of whether a given sentence S presupposes a sentence P. Let us look more closely at these two features of presupposition.

We define presupposition as follows: a sentence S *presupposes* a sentence P just in case S has truth-value zero whenever P is not true. Obviously, this definition is a direct generalization of the sort of situation we found to be the case in our example.

The rest of our discussion relies on the notion of entailment, and it is here that the somewhat non-standard definition of entailment that we made above comes into play: it works in a three-valued as well as a two-valued logic.

Suppose S presupposes P and S is true. Then from the definition of presupposition, P must be true as well, in which case it follows that S entails P. On the other hand, suppose that S is false. Then not-S is true, and also, P must be true. Thus not-S entails P as well. Hence if S presupposes P then both S and its negation entail P.

It happens that the converse of this law holds too. To see this, suppose that both S and not-S entail P. Assume that P is false. Then since S entails P, S cannot be true. Also, since not-S entails P, not-S cannot be true and consequently S cannot be false. Since S is neither true nor false, it must have zero as its truth-value. Hence S presupposes P.

We have now established that S presupposes P if both S and not-S entail P, from which it is an obvious consequence that S and not-S have exactly the same presuppositions, that is, that presupposition is constant under negation. The little theorem that we have established provides the basis for a very reliable and easy-to-apply criterion for deciding whether S presupposes P: simply determine whether both S and not-S entail P. If so, then S presupposes P; otherwise S does not presuppose P.

Many other semantic criteria for presupposition are suggested and discussed in Kiparsky and Kiparsky (1971) and in Karttunen (1972); all are of somewhat less importance than the criteria of constancy under negation. Two of these criteria in particular, however, are quite useful, convincing, and easy to apply, so we present them below.

The first criterion is the constancy of presupposition under transformation of indicatives to interrogatives. The following examples should suffice to illustrate and justify this principle:

A.   It is sad that the money is gone.
A'. Isn't it sad that the money is gone?
B.   John is dismayed that the money is gone.
B'. Is John dismayed that the money is gone?
C.   He is sure that the money is gone.
C'. Is he sure that the money is gone?
D.   It is possible that the money is gone.
D'. Isn't it possible that the money is gone?

A quick check of A, B, C, and D should serve to show that A and B presuppose that the money is gone, while C and D do not. Now note that in questions A' and B', it is taken for granted that the money is gone, and the questions involve some sort of reflection on this state of affairs. In contrast, the point of questions C' and D' is some sort of reflection on whether the money indeed *is* gone. If in fact the money is not gone, then A' and B' are infelicitous along just the same lines as the classic example of an infelicitous question "When did you stop beating your wife?", when in fact the wife was never beaten. But this is *not* the case for questions C' and D'. These questions are fine whether the money is really gone or not. In short, then, we see from these examples that presupposition carries over into interrogatives.

The final semantic criterion of presupposition (due to Karttunen [1972]) we mention is that presupposition is not disturbed when sentences are complemented by modal operators. Again we illustrate with some examples:

A". It is possible that it is sad that the money is gone.
B". It must be that John is dismayed that the money is gone.

C''. It must be that he is sure that the money is gone.
D''. It must be possible that the money is gone.

The sentences which presuppose that the money is gone are A''
and B'', while C'' and D'' do not presuppose this. This is so even
though A'' does *not* presuppose that it is sad that the money is
gone. We therefore take constancy of presupposition under com-
plementation by modal operators as our third semantic criterion
of presupposition.

6.1.2.3 *The Factive Thesis*

Kiparsky and Kiparsky argue that factivity and presupposition
are correlated. Their position is summed up in the following
passage:

> The force of the *that*-clause is not the same in the two sentences
>   It is odd that it is raining (factive)
>   It is likely that it is raining (non-factive)
> or in the two sentences
>   I regret that it is raining (factive)
>   I suppose that it is raining (non-factive).
> The first sentence in each pair (the factive sentence) carries with
> it the presupposition 'it is raining'. The speaker presupposes that
> the embedded clause expresses a true proposition, and makes
> some assertion about that proposition. All predicates which be-
> have syntactically as factives have this property, and almost none
> of those which behave syntactically as non-factives have it. This,
> we propose, is the basic difference between the two types of
> predicates (Kiparsky and Kiparsky 1971, 348).

The connection between the *syntactic* characteristic of factivity
and the *semantic* characteristic of presupposition is summed up
in the following principle, which I call the *factive thesis*:

> Factive Thesis: Sentences whose main predicates are sentence-
> complementing presuppose their complements if and almost only
> if the predicates are factives.

(The reason for the qualification "almost" in this thesis is considered below.)

The only way to test this thesis is to check a large sample of its instances. Obviously everyone who has written on this topic has gone through this exercise, and the reader is invited to do the same. As a start, it might be pointed out that many of the examples already used in this chapter may be seen to conform to the hypothesis. Furthermore, we will now check two arbitrarily chosen predicates, one factive, one not, for illustrative purposes.

We will consider the predicates 'conjecture' and 'reveal to'. We first apply syntactic criteria to determine factivity or non-factivity, starting with constructions employing 'fact'. Consider the following:

*Goldbach conjectured the fact that every even number greater than two is the sum of two primes.

*Descartes conjectured the fact of the pituitary gland being the seat of intelligence.

Einstein revealed to us all the fact that the geometry of space is non-Euclidean.

The ghost revealed to Hamlet the fact of his father's having been murdered by his uncle.

On this criterion, 'conjecture' seems to be a non-factive and 'reveal to' a factive predicate.

The next criterion involves gerundial constructions and adjectival nominalizations in -ness. Again we consider examples:

*We all conjectured the pricelessness of the gift.

*Othello conjectured the scheming of Cassio.

Tom revealed to Sue the pricelessness of the gift.

Iago revealed to Othello the scheming of Cassio.

Again, the syntactic evidence favors the factivity of 'revealed to' and the non-factivity of 'conjectured'.

The final syntactic criterion of factivity (extraposition does not apply because neither predicate is one-place) involves the accusative and infinitive construction:

Sagan conjectures there to be millions of civilizations in the universe.

*Voyager revealed to science there to be thousands of rings around Saturn.

The first sentence I find only marginally acceptable, but not every non-factive sentence is allowable in this construction anyway, so this does not disturb our conclusion that 'conjecture' is a non-factive. On the other hand, the second sentence is clearly unacceptable, so all the evidence indicates that 'reveals to' is a factive predicate.

Our task is now to use the semantic criterion of presupposition to see whether sentences employing "reveals to" presuppose their complements while those employing "conjecture" do not. We begin by checking whether sentences using these verbs entail their complements, and furthermore, whether this entailment is constant under negation. We begin with 'conjecture':

P: Sagan conjectures that there are millions of advanced civilizations.
Q: There are millions of advanced civilizations.

It seems rather obvious that P does not entail Q, and a counter-example is readily available. In fact, Sagan *has* conjectured that there are millions of advanced civilizations in the universe, and certainly he may be completely wrong. We may be the only civilization in the universe, in which case there are no advanced civilizations at all. If this is so, then P is true and Q false, so P does not entail Q. Hence P cannot presuppose Q either.

Let us now turn to the much more interesting case of 'reveal to', and consider the following example:

P: The ghost revealed to Hamlet that Hamlet's father was murdered.
Q: Hamlet's father was murdered.

One is inclined to say that P entails Q. For if Q were false, then the ghost could not *reveal* to Hamlet that his father was murdered—the ghost might *tell* Hamlet this, or *claim* it, but not *reveal* it. To bolster this assertion, we apply the inconsistency and consistency tests.

\# The ghost revealed to Hamlet that Hamlet's father was murdered and Hamlet's father was not murdered.

? The ghost revealed to Hamlet that Hamlet's father was murdered and Hamlet's father was murdered.

Hamlet's father was murdered and the ghost revealed to Hamlet that Hamlet's father was murdered.

The third sentence is included here for contrast with the second. A clear performance oddity is exhibited by the second sentence, and at least some felt inconsistency is associated with the first. We conclude that P does entail Q.

We now must determine whether this entailment persists under negation, so we must test whether not-P entails Q as well, where

not-P: The ghost did not reveal to Hamlet that Hamlet's father was murdered.

It happens that in this case it appears more intuitively clear that not-P entails Q than it does that P entails Q, but we nonetheless apply the consistency and inconsistency tests:

\# The ghost did not reveal to Hamlet that Hamlet's father was murdered and Hamlet's father was not murdered.

? The ghost did not reveal to Hamlet that Hamlet's father was murdered and Hamlet's father was murdered.

Hamlet's father was murdered and the ghost did not reveal to Hamlet that Hamlet's father was murdered.

The felt inconsistency of the first sentence apparently hinges on the word 'reveal'. If Hamlet's father indeed was *not* murdered, then the ghost could hardly fail to *reveal* that he was murdered. The ghost might not *claim* that Hamlet's father was murdered (*ergo* a sincere ghost), but it is beyond even the power of a ghost to fail to reveal something which is not the case. Likewise the second sentence exhibits a performance oddity hinging on 're- veal', as contrast with the third sentence makes evident. So we conclude that both P and not-P entail Q, and that therefore P presupposes Q.

To complete our examination of 'reveal,' we present interrog- atives and modal sentences to reinforce our tentative conclusion that sentences employing 'reveal to' presuppose their complements.

Did Voyager reveal to us that Titan has a nitrogen atmosphere?

It is necessary that penitents reveal to their confessors that they have sinned.

Is it possible that the police will reveal to the public that dozens of thefts have occurred?

Note in these examples that presupposition is constant under the addition of modal operators, and that the questions become infelicitous if the appropriate complement sentence is false. Thus our conclusion regarding 'reveal to' has been verified.

We have now established that 'conjecture' is a non-factive predicate and furthermore that sentences employing this verb in the main clause do not presuppose their complements. In contrast, 'reveal to' is a factive predicate and sentences in which this verb is used in the main clause presuppose their comple- ments. Thus we have verified, for two instances, Kiparsky and Kiparsky's claim (i.e., the factive thesis) that sentences whose main predicates are sentence-complementing presuppose their complements if and (almost) only if the predicates are factives.

6.1.2.4 Complications

There are two important complications of Kiparsky and Ki- parsky's position that must be noted. Each has a share in forcing the word 'almost' to appear in the factive thesis.

The first reason for introducing 'almost' is that there exists a small class of words which are non-factive but which appear to presuppose their complements. Kiparsky and Kiparsky cite 'know' as the paradigm of this class. In the next section we will argue that Kiparsky and Kiparsky are mistaken about this class of terms—that they do not in fact *presuppose* their complements though they do *entail* them. Thus one reason for restricting the above conclusion will be removed. The second reason, however, cannot be removed.

The second reason for including 'almost' in the factive thesis concerns the simple division of sentence-complementing words into two mutually exclusive and exhaustive classes of factive and non-factive predicates. This turns out to be too simple, because there are predicates which may occur in both factive and non-factive syntactic constructions. Although troublesome, this state of affairs does not violate the factive/non-factive distinction, nor is it particularly anomalous. For there are analogous cases regarding other grammatical distinctions in which the same sort of thing occurs. Kiparsky and Kiparsky point out that

> this is analogous to the fact that there are not only verbs which take abstract objects but also verbs which take either kind. For example, *hit* requires concrete objects (*boy, table*), *clarify* requires abstract objects (*ideas, fact*), and *like* occurs indifferently with both. Just so we find verbs which occur indifferently with factive and non-factive complements, e.g. *anticipate, acknowledge, suspect, report, remember, emphasize, announce, admit, deduce*. Such verbs have no specification in the lexicon as to whether their complements are factive. On a deeper level, their semantic representations include no specifications as to whether their complement sentences represent presuppositions by the speaker or not. Syntactically, these sentences participate in both complement paradigms (Kiparsky and Kiparsky 1971, 360).

(By the phrase "factive and non-factive complements," Kiparsky and Kiparsky mean complement phrases whose syntactic structures characteristically occur with factive or non-factive verbs, respectively.) To illustrate that these terms are indifferent to factive or non-factive complements, we arbitrarily choose 'remember' to provide some examples. The following are constructions in which non-factive predicates (usually) may not occur:

> We remember the fact that rabbits were terrorizing the neighborhood.

> John remembers the happiness at the wake.

> She remembers the relabeling of the bottles.

Hence 'remember' may take factive complements. On the other hand, consider the following example, in which factive verbs may not occur:

> She remembers Nixon to be a crook.

This sentence is perfectly acceptable, hence 'remember' is neither a factive nor a non-factive predicate. We will call this class of predicates the *syntactically indifferent* or just *indifferent* predicates.

It is interesting to note that a sentence employing a syntactically indifferent predicate in its main clause presupposes its complement if the syntactic form of the complement is factive, that is, if it is one of the constructions disallowed for non-factive predicates. Kiparsky and Kiparsky illustrate this as follows:

> Compare, for example, the two sentences
>> They reported the enemy to have suffered a decisive defeat.
>> They reported the enemy's having suffered a decisive defeat.
> The second implies that the report was true in the speaker's opinion, while the first leaves open the possibility that the report was false . . . Similarly, compare
>> I remembered him to be bald (so I was surprised to see him with long hair).
>> I remembered his being bald (so I brought along a wig and disguised him).
> (Kiparsky and Kiparsky 1971, 360).

Hence the connection between syntactic form and (semantic) presupposition holds even for the class of indifferent predicates.

This completes our review of factives. We can summarize its main points as follows: among sentence-complementing terms, we may distinguish three mutually exclusive and exhaustive classes purely on syntactic grounds. The factive predicates accept complements employing the head noun 'fact', gerundial constructions, and adjectival nominalizations in -*ness*, but they do not accept complements employing infinitive constructions. The non-factive predicates, on the other hand, mostly admit infinitive constructions but not the others. Finally, the class of syntactically indifferent predicates can accept complement sentences in any of these syntactic categories.

A semantic distinction accompanies these syntactic differences. The factive thesis states that sentences whose main predicates are factive presuppose their complements; sentences whose main predicates are non-factive do not (generally) presuppose their complements; sentences whose main predicates are syntactically indifferent presuppose their complements only if the complement employs one of the distinctively factive constructions.

6.1.3 Assertives

Kiparsky and Kiparsky would like to claim that sentences employing factive predicates in their main clause presuppose their complements, while those employing non-factive predicates do not. They believe, however, that there are exceptions to the latter part of this claim. In particular, they claim that "verbs like *know*, *realize*, though semantically factive [i.e. sentences employing these verbs presuppose their complements], are syntactically non-factive" (Kiparsky and Kiparsky 1971, 348). In this section, we argue that though 'know' and 'realize' indeed are syntactically non-factive, they are not "semantically factive" as Kiparsky and Kiparsky believe. Thus the second part of the claim listed above can be maintained after all. Furthermore, a closer look at why words like 'know' and 'realize' appear to be "semantically factive" leads to a further distinction within the classes of non-factive and syntactically indifferent terms between those predicates which, when used in the main clause of a sentence, cause the entailment of the complement sentence and those which do not. This latter distinction is important for our purposes, so we coin the term 'assertives' to apply to the former and 'non-as-sertives' to the latter class.

In disputing Kiparsky and Kiparsky's claim that there are pred-icates which are syntactically non-factive but nevertheless se-mantically factive, we will focus on the verb 'know,' mostly because it is already the favorite example in the literature. How-ever the discussion will apply to several other predicates, in-cluding 'realize', and a few more, as the reader is invited to verify for himself or herself.

I first establish that 'know' is syntactically non-factive; we quote Kiparsky and Kiparsky in this regard:

> we cannot say
>   *I know the fact that John is here,
>   *I know John's being here,
> whereas the propositional [infinitive]
> constructions are acceptable:
>   I know him to be here
> (Kiparsky and Kiparsky 1971, 348).

Thus 'know' cannot be used in those syntactic structures re-served for factives, but can be used in those where factives are unacceptable. It follows that 'know' is non-factive.

For arguments to the effect that 'know' is not semantically factive we turn to a note by Deirdre Wilson (1972). In her note, Wilson attempts to call into question Kiparsky and Kiparsky's thesis that sentences employing factive verbs presuppose their complements. She bases her argument on examples employing 'know' and shows convincingly that presupposition does not occur. She concludes that since 'know' is a factive, factive pred-icates do not introduce presupposition as claimed. Wilson's ar-gument breaks down, of course, because 'know' in fact is a non-factive, as Kiparsky and Kiparsky explicitly state. Wilson con-fuses being syntactically factive with being semantically factive (which is understandable—this latter term is really quite con-fusing, although it is more convenient than the more precise but long-winded locution regarding sentences presupposing their complements). The thing that Wilson does succeed in establish-ing, however, is exactly what we wish to show at this point, namely that Kiparsky and Kiparsky's claim that 'know' is semantically factive is wrong. Hence we recount Wilson's arguments below.

Wilson notes that if a sentence S presupposes a sentence Q, but Q is false, then S lacks a truth-value, or has a zero or indeterminate truth-value. On the other hand, if S entails Q but does not presuppose Q, then if Q is false, so is S. With this in mind, Wilson asks us to consider the following argument:

Premise 1:   No one knows (can know) that Nixon is bald unless Nixon is bald.
Premise 2:   Nixon is not bald.
Conclusion 1: No one knows (can know) that Nixon is bald. (from P1,P2).
Premise 3:   John is a person.
Conclusion 2: John does not know that Nixon is bald. (from P3, P1, P2, via C1)

(Wilson 1972, 406).

On the basis of this argument, Wilson urges that factives cannot require presupposition as follows:

> The point is that Conclusion 2 is deduced from Premise 2, among others. Conclusion 2 is a factive sentence with a complement, and Premise 2 is the negation of that complement. Thus the truth of Conclusion 2 follows from the assumption that its complement is false. But it clearly makes no sense to talk of Conclusion 2 as presupposing the truth of its complement when in fact it follows logically from its falsity. . . . it follows that Conclusion 2, a factive, not only does not, but cannot presuppose the truth of its complement (Wilson 1972, 406–407).

If Wilson's argument is acceptable, then her claim that Conclusion 2 cannot presuppose its complement is unavoidable. And indeed the argument does appear to be perfectly acceptable, having, as Wilson claims, fully grammatical, true premises and a fully grammatical, true conclusion following deductively from the premises. So it appears that 'know' is not semantically factive.

A further important feature of this situation is brought out by Wilson. The truth of Premise 1 can be accounted for by the realization that the sentence

John knows that Nixon is bald.

entails its complement. Consequently, if the complement is false, it cannot be that John (or anyone else) knows that Nixon is bald. But this means that Premise 1 must be the case. Hence we have good reason to suppose that sentences in which 'know' is the main predicate entail their complements.

Before going on to consider further arguments for both of these conclusions regarding sentences employing 'know,' a subtle point regarding presupposition and entailment must be emphasized. If S presupposes Q, then S entails Q. The difference between entailment and presupposition arises regarding the *negation* of S. For if S presupposes Q, then not-S also entails Q. However, if S entails Q but does not presuppose Q, then not-S does not entail Q. Applying these generalizations to the case of John's knowing Nixon to be bald, we have the following: given that 'John knows that Nixon is bald' entails 'Nixon is bald' (which is the case whether we have presupposition or not) the question is whether 'John does not know that Nixon is bald' entails 'Nixon is bald'. If so, then presupposition is present, and if not there is entailment without presupposition. Wilson's argument shows that 'John does not know that Nixon is bald' *does not* entail 'Nixon is bald'. Hence there is entailment without presupposition.

To buttress her position, Wilson goes on to apply the consistency test of entailment to some examples, which she numbers as follows:

(1) John knows that Nixon is bald.
(2) John doesn't know that Nixon is bald.
(3) Nixon is bald.

According to the consistency test,

> if . . . (1) entails (3), and (2) does not entail (3), we would expect the conjunction of (1) and (3) to result in a performance oddity, and the conjunction of (2) and (3) not to. On the other hand, if (1) and (2) both presuppose (3), we would expect the conjunctions of (1) and (3) and (2) and (3) to be equally acceptable or odd. I think that there is indeed a difference in acceptability between

the conjunctions, which implies that the relevant relation is entailment and not presupposition:

(6) ?John knows that Nixon is bald but (and) Nixon is bald.

(7) John doesn't know that Nixon is bald but (and) Nixon is bald.

Clearly (7) is much better with *but* instead of *and*. The fact that . . . (6) . . . [is] markedly worse with *but* instead of *and* further supports [the conclusion] (Wilson 1972, 408).

Thus the consistency test supports Wilson in her conclusions on both counts.

It is now clear that 'know' is not "semantically factive," and we may wonder why Kiparsky and Kiparsky think it (and several other verbs as well) is semantically factive. An explanation is forthcoming in terms of certain other features of 'know' and Grice's maxims governing conversation. To begin with the former, it is commonly held that a claim of the form 'X knows that P' (where X is a person and P a sentence), at least entails that P is true, that X believes that P, and that X has adequate grounds for believing that P.[†] If this analysis of 'know' is correct, then failure of just one of these conditions will force the knowledge claim to be false, and its negation to be true. Hence the claim that X doesn't know that P may be true by virtue of the falsity of one, two, or all three of the conditions enumerated above. What's more, crucially, claims of the form 'X doesn't know that P' do not in any way indicate which condition(s) fail(s). The denial that X knows that P may be true because in fact p is false, or because p is true but X doesn't believe it, or because p is false and X doesn't believe it anyway, and so on.

With this in mind, let us consider what sorts of assertions would be made in denying X's knowledge that P under the constraint of Grice's maxims. Suppose the topic of discussion is whether Harvey is a thief, and if so, whether Adele knows it. If it is desired to assert that Harvey is not a thief, and so Adele can't know that he is, one might say either of the following:

† See (Lehrer 1974) for a typical discussion of this position.

A.   Harvey is not a thief (and so Adele doesn't know it).

B.   Adele doesn't know that Harvey is a thief.

However, if one asserts B, then it is ambiguous whether Adele doesn't know that Harvey is a thief because he's not or because he is but she isn't aware of it. The first Gricean maxim requires that a speaker be just as informative as is required for present purposes. If sentence B is asserted, then, the maxim dictates that the assertion be understood in the second way mentioned. For if the first way is meant, then the maxim is violated because in that case sentence A is more informative than B. Thus assertions like B, (i.e., denials of knowledge claims) are ambiguous but are conventionally understood (barring contextual clues to the contrary) to assert that the subject lacks an appropriate belief-state rather than that the proposition in question is false. Employing Gricean terminology, sentences of the form 'X doesn't know that P' are often taken to *conversationally* imply (though they do not *logically* imply) that P is true.

This being the case, it is not at all surprising that 'know' could be mistaken for a semantically factive predicate. For recall that the primary test of presupposition is whether it is constant under negation. Since, as we noted to start with, 'X knows that P' logically entails P, and as we have just discovered, 'X doesn't know that P' often conversationally entails P, there is a strong temptation to conclude that 'X knows that P' presupposes P. This mistake is particularly likely to occur when no distinction is made between logical and conversational entailment, and where presupposition is not clearly characterized as a logical (as opposed, for example, to a psychological) relation between sentences. Kiparsky and Kiparsky in fact don't make these distinctions.

Finally, the same sort of subtlety and confusion arises with regard to the other tests of presupposition that we have mentioned, namely the constancy of presupposition under conversion to an interrogative, and the constancy of presupposition under addition of modal operators. Thus there is good reason for 'know' (and the other verbs mentioned by Kiparsky and

Kiparsky) to be mistaken for a semantically factive predicate, though it is not one.

We conclude regarding 'know' that (i) it is a (syntactically) non-factive predicate; (ii) it is not "semantically factive," meaning that sentences in which 'know' is the main predicate do not presuppose their complements; and (iii) sentences in which 'know' is the main predicate do entail their complements (without presupposing them). Examination of other allegedly syntactically non-factive but semantically factive predicates, like 'realize', yield the same conclusions. Therefore Kiparsky and Kiparsky are incorrect in their belief that some non-factive verbs cause presupposition of complement sentences.

Although sentences employing 'know' and 'realize' in the main clause do not presuppose their complements, we have found that they *do* entail their complements. We are thus led to distinguish between such predicates, which we call *assertives*, and predicates which, when used in the main clause of a sentence, do not cause any entailments. The latter predicates we term *non-assertive*.

Since assertives cause entailment but no presupposition and non-assertives cause no entailments at all, it must be the case that all assertives and non-assertives are not factive; that is, they are all drawn from the classes of non-factive and syntactically indifferent predicates.

So far we have seen only examples of non-factive assertive predicates, and these required considerable effort in demonstrating that they were indeed assertives. We therefore fill out our account with less controversial examples and examples of other sorts of assertives. For three non-controversial examples of non-factive assertive predicates, consider 'true', 'necessary', and 'correct'. These have already been established to be non-factive, and clearly sentences of the form

It's true that P.

It's necessary that P.

It's correct that P.

X is correct that P.

all entail P. In fact we may take 'true' as the paradigm non-factive assertive because of its non-controversiality in all respects.

The following are non-factive non-assertive predicates, as the reader may readily verify:

possible	sure	think
unnecessary	appears	believe
likely	conjecture	remark

Relying on modal logic to verify our logical intuitions and previous discussion to establish non-factivity, we may take 'possible' as the paradigm of the non-factive non-assertive predicates.

Turning to the class of syntactically indifferent predicates, we find that an elaboration of our position is required. In our discussion of indifferent predicates, we mentioned Kiparsky and Kiparsky's finding that a sentence employing a syntactically indifferent predicate in its main clause presupposes its complement if the syntactic form of the complement is one of those only allowed with factive (or indifferent) predicates. But if a predicate is an assertive then it causes complement sentences to be entailed, not presupposed. Hence it is inconsistent to claim that there are assertive or non-assertive indifferent predicates. This difficulty is overcome by qualifying the definitions of assertive and non-assertive predicates as follows: a predicate is an *assertive* if either (i) it is non-factive and when it is used as the main predicate in a sentence, then the sentence entails but does not presuppose its complement or (ii) it is syntactically indifferent, and when it is used as the main predicate in a sentence whose complement does not have a syntactic form characteristic of factive predicates, then the sentence entails but does not presuppose its complement. The definition of a non-assertive predicate is altered in like fashion.

In later discussion, the classes of indifferent assertive and indifferent non-assertive predicates will be of little consequence. Hence it will suffice for our purposes to list samples of each class, leaving it to the reader to verify that these examples have the characteristics claimed for them.

The following are indifferent assertive predicates:

prove	deduce	discover
acknowledge	see	lucky
admit	notice	reveal (that)

The paradigm of this class is 'see'. The following are examples of indifferent non-assertive predicates: 'report' and 'suspect'. In this case 'report' is the paradigm example.

6.1.4 Counter-Assertives

So far in our discussion we have been solely concerned with the question whether various sentence-complementing terms, when used as the main predicate in a sentence P with complement sentence Q, cause P to entail Q. This is of interest because our eventual aim is to discover whether sentences of the form 'X informs Y that P' entail P. However we want also to discover whether sentences of the form 'X misinforms Y that P' entail not-P. Hence we must now consider whether various sentence-complementing terms, when used as the main predicate of P, cause P to entail the *negation* of Q.

Our initial investigation attacked the question about entailment by dividing the problem into cases where on the one hand there was both entailment with presupposition, and on the other hand where there was entailment without presupposition. One is inclined to pursue the question now under investigation in the same fashion; however, it turns out not to be necessary to pay much attention to sentence-complementing predicates which cause *presupposition* of the negation of complement sentences, because there don't appear to be any. It appears that there are no "counter-factive" predicates.

This fact is at first quite striking because it presents such a marked asymmetry in the grammar of our language. There are many factives and many assertives. As we will see, there are also several counter-assertives. One therefore expects that English will contain at least one or two counter-factives. However, for reasons that I have been unable to fathom, there simply do not seem to be any.

As noted, although there are no predicates which cause presupposition of the negation of complement sentences, there are predicates, which I call *counter-assertives*, which, when used as the main predicate in a sentence P with complement sentence Q, cause P to entail not-Q. Before presenting a list of counter-assertives, we can note a few important features of such words. First, by virtue of the definitions and discoveries made above, a counter-assertive obviously cannot be a factive, an assertive, or a non-assertive predicate. Furthermore, a counter-assertive cannot be a syntactically indifferent predicate. For suppose that some predicate F is an indifferent counter-assertive predicate. Then when F is used as the main predicate in sentences whose complement has one of the syntactic forms characteristically accepted by factives, the sentence will presuppose its complement. (Recall that this sort of behavior is characteristic of syntactically indifferent predicates.) On the other hand, since F is counter-assertive, it always causes entailment of the negation of the complement sentence. Thus in certain cases, a sentence employing F as its main predicate would entail both its complement and the negation of its complement, in which case it would be logically inconsistent. Hence the class of counter-assertive predicates cannot overlap the class of syntactically indifferent predicates.

We may thus conclude regarding the class of counter-assertive predicates that it is drawn from the class of non-factive predicates which are not non-assertive.

Having decided in general what sorts of predicates may inhabit the set of counter-assertives, we turn to specific examples:

| false | untrue | wrong |
| impossible | incorrect | lie (that) |

It is quite easy to establish that these predicates meet the definition of counter-assertives. Consider the three sentences:

A. It's false that Columbus discovered America.

B. It's not false that Columbus discovered America.

C. Columbus did not discover America.

Clearly A entails C (which is the negation of A's complement), and B (which is the negation of A) does not entail C. Hence A entails but does not presuppose the negation of its complement sentence C, so it is a counter-assertive. Cases for the other words in the list are likewise easily made.

This completes our typology of sentence-complementing words. In summary, we have partitioned this class into three subclasses on the basis of syntactic considerations, these subclasses being the factives, non-factives, and syntactically indifferent predicates. The factives all have the semantic property of causing presupposition of complement sentences. The non-factives are further partitioned on the basis of semantic features. Though non-factives never cause presupposition of complement sentences, they may cause entailment of complement sentences (assertives), entailment of the negations of complement sentences (counter-assertives), or no entailments (non-assertives). Thus there are three subclasses of non-factive predicates. The indifferent predicates are likewise partitioned on the basis of semantic features. When used in sentences where the complement has a syntactic form not characteristically accepted by factive predicates, indifferent predicates may still entail, without presupposing, complement sentences. If so, they are assertive, and otherwise, non-assertive. Thus the indifferent predicates have two subclasses.

6.2 INFORMING AND MISINFORMING

In this section, we determine whether 'inform' requires truth and whether 'misinform' requires falsity. This is accomplished by determining where these words fit in the typology of sentence-complementing words developed above.

Our first task is to determine the syntactic characteristics of 'inform', by applying the criteria of factivity. The first criterion involves replacing the *that*-clause by a construction consisting of 'the fact' followed by a simple *that*-clause or a gerund.

*The ghost informed Hamlet the fact that his uncle was a usurper.

The ghost revealed to Hamlet the fact that his uncle was a usurper.

*I informed her the fact of John's contracting hepatitis.

I revealed to her the fact of John's contracting hepatitis.

These constructions are accepted by all and only factives. We see that 'inform' cannot be used in this way while 'reveal', a three-place factive, can. Hence on this criterion, 'inform' is not factive.

The second criterion of factivity is to test whether the *that*-clause may be replaced by gerunds and adjectival nominalizations in -*ness*. Usually, only factive predicates are allowable in this construction.

*Sue informed me his being found guilty.

Sue revealed to me his being found guilty.

*Iago informed Othello the faithlessness of Desdemona.

Iago revealed to Othello the faithlessness of Desdemona.

When 'inform' is used in such constructions, the result is unacceptable, so according to this criterion, 'inform' is not factive.

The third criterion requires that we test to see whether 'inform' can be used with the infinitive-accusative construction. Factives, and some non-factives, do not allow this construction.

I informed her that John knows about it.

*I informed her John to know about it.

*I revealed to her John to know about it.

The first sentence is included to show the original *that*-clause which is replaced by the infinitive phrase. Since 'reveal' is a factive, the third sentence is unacceptable as expected. Unfortunately, the second sentence is also unacceptable, meaning that 'inform' is either factive or one of those non-factive (like 'possible' or 'true') that cannot be used in this construction.

The fourth criterion of factivity, involving extraposition, is not applicable because 'inform' is not a one-place predicate.

The results of applying the three appropriate criteria of factivity are that two clearly indicate that 'inform' is not factive and one gives an ambiguous indication. We conclude that 'inform' is not factive. Furthermore, since 'inform' cannot be used with complement sentences whose syntactic form is that characteristically employed with factive predicates, 'inform' is not syntactically indifferent either. Hence 'inform' is non-factive. Consequently, we may conclude that in no case does it cause presupposition of complement sentences.

Given that 'inform' is non-factive, we still must determine whether it is assertive, counter-assertive, or non-assertive. Presumably, it is *prima facie* absurd to suppose that 'inform' is counter-assertive. Consequently we need but determine whether 'inform' causes entailment (without presupposition, of course) of complement sentences. To decide this question, we employ the three tests of entailment.

The basic criterion for deciding whether an entailment obtains is carefully and thoughtfully to consult intuitions, giving special scrutiny to all sorts of examples, particularly counter-examples, if there are any. In this case, as was noted when the chapter began, intuitions do not provide very strong support for claims in either direction. However it does seem that rather convincing counter-examples are available. For example, consider the following sentence:

Dan Rather informed the nation that James Brady was dead.

Apparently, this sentence is true. There can be no doubt, however, that the complement sentence, 'James Brady was dead', is false. Hence we have a counter-example to the claim that 'inform' is an assertive, so 'inform' is a non-assertive predicate.

We can use the consistency and inconsistency tests to buttress this conclusion. According to the consistency test, if P entails Q then, and *only* then, the conjunction "P and Q" should exhibit a performance oddity. Furthermore, if the converse entailment fails, that is, if Q does not entail P then by contrast the conjunction "Q and P" should *not* exhibit a performance oddity. In application of this test, consider the following conjunctions:

A. Mary informed John that he was in arrears and he was in arrears.
B. John was in arrears and Mary informed him that he was in arrears.

Neither of these sentences exhibits a performance oddity. In particular, A is certainly not odd in any way, as would be the case if 'inform' were an assertive. Furthermore, sentence A has the sense of 'Mary informed John that he was in arrears, and furthermore, she was right'. In other words, the second conjunct of sentence A has the force of stating that the information Mary conveyed to John was true, supplementing what is claimed in the first conjunct. This is a clear indication that, as we thought, 'inform' is not an assertive predicate.

Finally, we come to the inconsistency test of entailment. Recall that according to this test, if P entails Q then there should be a felt inconsistency in asserting that 'P and not-Q', and otherwise there should not be. Consider the following examples:

C. Nixon informs us that he is not a crook and Nixon is a crook.
D. Sagan informed us that we are not alone, but we are alone.
E. The registrar informed Tom that he was admitted and he was not admitted.
F. He informed me that he was going to the party but then he didn't go.

There is no felt inconsistency in the assertion of sentences C, D, E, and F. Hence according to the inconsistency test, there is no entailment between the first conjuncts of these sentences and their complement sentence. By this test too, then, we are led to conclude that 'inform' is not assertive.

We have now determined that 'inform' is a non-factive, non-assertive predicate. As such, it is never the case that a sentence P, whose main predicate is 'inform', either presupposes, or entails without presupposing, its complement sentence Q. In other words, sentences of the form 'X informs Y that P' do not entail P. *Informing does not require truth.*

We turn now to the question of whether 'misinform' is a counter-assertive or non-assertive predicate. The answer must be sought by once again employing the criteria of entailment, this time to see whether sentences of the form 'X misinforms Y that P' entail not-P.

As a first step in our argument, we consider some examples as foci for the application of our logical intuitions.

G. Sagan misinforms us that there are millions of advanced civilizations in the universe.
H. Nixon misinforms us that he is not a crook.

Can it be that Sagan *misinforms* us, as sentence G claims, if indeed
there *are* millions of advanced civilizations in the universe? It
seems not. Likewise, if we have been wrong about Nixon all
these years, and he is really *not* a crook, as he claims, is H true?
Again, it seems not. The farce of sentences G and H appears to
be that the informer (or misinformer) is making a false claim.
Hence our tentative conclusion regarding 'misinform' is that it
is a counter-assertive predicate.

As examples for the application of the consistency test, consider the following:

? Mary misinformed John that Florence did it and Florence did not
do it.

Florence did not do it and Mary misinformed John that Florence
did it.

? She misinformed me that the truth was out and the truth was not
out.

The truth was not out and she misinformed me that the truth
was out.

It seems that the first and third of these examples exhibit slight
performance oddities. These oddities are not as striking as those
exhibited in examples considered earlier, so it only seems safe
to regard the consistency test as giving weak support to our
hypothesis that 'misinform' is a counter-assertive. Nevertheless,
this test does give some support to the hypothesis.

We come now to the inconsistency test and consider the following conjunctions:

Agnes misinformed Harry that the cat was dead and the cat was
dead.

\# Galileo misinformed us that Jupiter has moons and Jupiter has moons.

\# He misinformed the class that pi is irrational and pi is irrational.

This test does give strong results. All three examples engender felt inconsistency, prompting the conclusion that the first conjunct entails the second. Consequently we are confirmed in our conclusion that 'misinform' is a counter-assertive predicate.

In summary, logical intuitions urge that 'misinform' is a counter-assertive predicate, and although the consistency test fails to give firm results in confirmation of this hypothesis, the inconsistency test does provide strong evidence in its support. We therefore conclude that 'misinform' is a counter-assertive predicate. In other words, sentences of the form 'X misinforms Y that P' entail not-P. *Misinforming requires falsity.*

In reviewing the conclusions of this section, we find that another asymmetry in our language has been discovered. When investigating factives and assertives, it was discovered that there are counter-assertives but no counter-factives. It has now been discovered that 'inform' and 'misinform', often taken as exact opposites, are not strict antonyms after all. If P is false, and X tells Y that P, then it is correct to say both that X informs Y that P *and* that X misinforms Y that P. On the other hand, if P is true, then X informs Y that P but X does not misinform Y that P. Thus misinforming is a kind of informing rather than a fundamentally different sort of activity.

There is a certain lingering, counter-intuitive flavor to these results. It still seems that a claim to the effect that X informs Y that P has about it the suggestion that P is true, rather than being indifferent about the truth of P, as we might expect. To account for this, we appeal once more to Grice's maxims governing conversation. Recall that the first of the maxims is to "be as informative (but no more so), than is required," and the fourth to "be brief, clear and orderly." In situations in which one is inclined to state that X has told Y that P, it is generally, or at least often, to the point to indicate as well whether P is true or false. If P is believed to be false, then in accordance with maxims (1) and (4), it is most appropriate to use 'misinform', since this carries with it the proper aspersions regarding the truth of P. More specifically, if 'inform' were used in lieu of 'misinform' when P is believed to be false, then either one would not be as informative as is required by maxim (1), or one would be obliged to state further that P is false, which violates maxim (4). Thus, in general, if the speaker believes P to be false, it is proper and conventional to use 'misinform'. Otherwise (meaning those cases in which, to the best of the speaker's knowledge, P is true), one uses 'inform'. By default, then, 'inform' is generally associated with truth (or with information believed to be true). Thus there is a perfectly reasonable explanation for the traditional associations between informing and truth, and misinforming and falsehood even though the former association is not a semantic feature of 'inform'.

6.3 CONCLUSION

Although a long and involved argument was required, we have now established firm answers to the two questions that we set out to answer in this chapter. Recall that these questions are the following:

1. Do sentences of the form 'X informs Y that P' entail P?
2. Do sentences of the form 'X misinforms Y that P' entail not-P?

The answer to the first question is that the entailment in question does *not* obtain; informing does not require truth. However, the answer to the second question is just the opposite: the entailment in question *does* obtain; misinforming does require falsity.

In terms of the consequences of these findings for the eventual analysis of 'inform' and 'misinform' (presented in Chapter 8 below), it is clear that a truth condition will not have to be included in the analysis of 'inform', while a falsity condition will have to be included in the analysis of 'misinform'. In other words, our analysis of 'misinform' must have the consequence that

X *misinforms* Y that P only if p is false.

In fact, on the assumption that misinforming differs from informing only with respect to their connections to truth, we may present a complete analysis of misinforming already:

X *misinforms* Y that P if
    1. X informs Y that P, and
    2. p is false.

Of course, this analysis will only be adequate when we have also provided an analysis of 'inform'.

This completes our investigation of informing, misinforming, and truth. Our conclusions will not figure in the discussion of information and belief in the next chapter, but they will be invoked when our investigation of 'inform' and 'misinform' is completed in Chapter 8 with analyses of these two notions.

7
INFORMING AND BELIEVING

There is reason to suspect that informing and believing are systematically related. One of the most important ways that people come to believe things is through having been informed by someone else that they are so. Consequently one may wonder whether one of the things involved in the process that occurs when X informs Y that P is that Y believes, or comes to believe, that P.

Likewise, one wonders whether X must believe that P in order to inform Y that P. For one does not associate informing with telling falsehoods, or making misleading statements; one's feeling is that informing is a privileged or special sort of telling, and that telling someone something that one doesn't believe doesn't fit the mold of informing.

In this chapter, then, I take up the questions of whether belief on the part of the informant or the informee are required for informing to take place. On the model used in the previous chapter, these questions can be framed in more precise fashion as follows:

1. Do sentences of the form 'X informs Y that P' entail those of the form 'X believes that P'?
2. Do sentences of the form 'X informs Y that P' entail those of the form 'Y believes that P'?

In contrast to the course followed in the last chapter, I will not pursue an extensive general investigation of sentence-complementing terms which cause the entailment of belief sentences, mainly because there is no such general theory. Even so, such an investigation is not really needed in the present case. It will be possible, I believe, to establish firm answers to the questions under investigation without resorting to much involved reasoning, for it turns out that there are quite convincing counter-examples showing that neither of the entailments in question obtain. Also the consistency and inconsistency tests provide straightforward corroborating evidence in favor of this conclusion.

7.1 BELIEF ON THE PART OF THE INFORMANT

In this section I argue that informing does not require belief on the part of the informant, that is, that sentences of the form 'X informs Y that P' do not entail the corresponding sentences 'X believes that P'. In defense of this claim, I present two examples of informing in which the informant does not believe what he or she is saying, and I apply the consistency and inconsistency tests of entailment to buttress this claim.

The first counter-example involves an informant who makes official pronouncements as part of his job, and consequently is in a position to inform people that P, whether he believes that P or not. Suppose that Jones is the Press-Secretary in the administration of a (fictional) president of the U.S. Imagine that this administration makes a habit of doing shady, immoral, illegal, and just plain mean things, and then lying about it. Secretary Jones knows this, and has no qualms about making claims to the press which he doesn't believe to be true. Now suppose that in response to allegations that the administration takes kickbacks from defense contractors, Jones is instructed to hold a press conference and to deny the accusations categorically. Although, we may suppose, it happens to be true that the administration is entirely free of this sort of corruption, Jones doesn't know this, and in fact he rather suspects that the accusations are true. In any case, Jones doesn't believe that the administration is innocent of taking kickbacks. Nevertheless, Jones holds a press conference and announces "No one in the administration has, is, or ever will accept any kickbacks or payoffs from any defense contractors."

The question is: has Jones informed the press that the administration is innocent of taking kickbacks? I trust that the reader will agree that the answer to this question is clearly "yes." Jones' job is to inform the press about the administration's positions and to answer questions about them. In carrying out these duties, Jones may inform the press that P regardless of his personal belief about p. Thus, in the example, Jones informs the press that the administration hasn't taken kickbacks (and furthermore he *correctly* so informs them), despite the fact that Jones does not himself believe this to be the case.

The second counter-example shows that someone may inform another that P without believing that P even though the informant does not do so in any official capacity. Suppose that Smith is a doctoral student who has been working for years on her dissertation. At a meeting to evaluate her progress, Smith informs her committee that she will definitely finish in three months' time. It happens that, in fact, Smith will finish in three months, although at the time of the meeting, Smith doesn't sincerely believe this to be the case. I submit that Smith *does* inform her committee that she will finish in three months, even though Smith herself doesn't believe it.

Both of the counter-examples exhibit cases in which it is true (making the appropriate substitutions for X, Y, and P) that X informs Y that P but false that X believes that P. Hence belief on the part of the informant must not be necessary for informing to take place. Further evidence on behalf of this conclusion is provided by the consistency and inconsistency tests.

Recall that, according to the inconsistency test, if P entails Q then there should be a "felt inconsistency" in asserting that both P and not-Q, and otherwise there should not be. Thus, to apply the inconsistency test, we consider some examples in which it is claimed that X informs Y that P but X does not believe that P. To help sharpen our intuitions, I include some examples of sentences which do clearly entail corresponding belief sentences.

John informs his mother that Tom hit Lisa, but John doesn't believe that Tom hit Lisa.

#John knows that Tom hit Lisa, but John doesn't believe that Tom hit Lisa.

The professor informed his colleagues that his discovery was sure to have many practical consequences, but the professor didn't believe that his discovery was sure to have many practical consequences.

The professor was certain that his discovery would have many practical consequences, but he didn't believe that it would have many practical consequences.

The doctor informed Herbert that his appendix was to blame, but the doctor didn't believe that Herbert's appendix was to blame.

The doctor decided that Herbert's appendix was to blame, but he didn't believe that Herbert's appendix was to blame.

The results of the inconsistency test are not ambiguous at all: there is no hint of inconsistency in the cases of the sentences employing 'inform', but rather blatant inconsistency in the other examples. This means that, as claimed, sentences of the form 'X informs Y that P' do not entail those of the form 'X believes that P'.

Finally, we come to the consistency test. In this test, an attempt is made to determine whether P entails Q by considering whether examples of the conjunction of P and Q exhibit a so-called performance oddity. As with the inconsistency test, examples where an entailment does obtain (and thus where a performance oddity is exhibited), are included to contrast with examples using the term 'inform.'

? John knew that Florence did it and John believed that Florence did it.

John informed Harriet that Florence did it, and John believed that Florence did it.

? Leo was certain that he had discovered a proof of Goldbach's conjecture, and Leo believed that he had discovered a proof of Goldbach's conjecture.

Leo informed me that he had discovered a proof of Goldbach's conjecture, and Leo believed that he had discovered a proof of Goldbach's conjecture.

? The judge thought that the defendant would serve a life sentence, and the judge believed that the defendant would serve a life sentence.

The judge informed the defendant that he would serve a life sentence, and the judge believed that the defendant would serve a life sentence.

The results of this test, like the results of the last, are quite clear-cut. The sentences employing 'inform' do not exhibit performance oddities, while those introduced to help focus our intuitions decidedly do exhibit such oddities. Hence, according to the consistency test, the entailment at issue does not obtain.

The conclusion of this section, then, is that belief on the part of the informant is not required for informing to take place. In other words, the answer to the first question enumerated above is that it is *not* the case that sentences of the form 'X informs Y that P' entail the corresponding belief sentences 'X believes that P'.

7.2 BELIEF ON THE PART OF THE INFORMEE

We now turn to the second question under consideration in this chapter, namely whether informing requires belief on the part of the informee, or, in other words, whether sentences of the form 'X informs Y that P' entail 'Y believes that P'. I claim that such belief is not required, and in support of this thesis I present, as in the last section, two counter-examples plus evidence from the consistency and inconsistency tests.

The first example makes use of a paradigm case of informing, namely what occurs when an arresting officer informs the person being arrested of his or her rights under the law. Suppose that Officer Jones arrests Smith, who does not know much about the Constitution. Officer Jones tells Smith that he has the right to remain silent, that he has a right to legal counsel, and so on. Smith, however, doesn't believe that he has these rights at all; perhaps he suspects that Jones is saying what he is saying in a subtle effort to trick him in some fashion.

Despite Smith's lack of belief in what Jones tells him, Officer Jones has nonetheless done his duty to *inform* Smith of his rights.

Jones is not responsible for seeing to it that Smith actually believes that he has the rights that Jones tells him about—Jones is
only responsible for telling Jones that he has these rights. Thus
Jones informs Smith that he has certain rights, even though
Smith does not believe that he does have these rights.

The second counter-example is more mundane than the first,
and so, perhaps, more persuasive. Suppose that vandals set
Jones' car on fire one night. Jones' roommate Smith happens to
look out the window and see that the car is on fire. Smith yells
to Jones that his car is on fire and rushes into the next room to
call the fire department. Jones, however, thinks that Smith (a
great practical joker) is just trying to get a rise out of him, and
hence Jones doesn't believe that his car is on fire (at least until
Smith can persuade him to look out the window). Nevertheless,
it is clear that Smith informs Jones that his car is on fire.

We thus have two clear instances in which it is true (making
the appropriate substitutions for X, Y, and P) that X informs Y
that P, but Y does not believe that P. Therefore it cannot be the
case that belief on the part of the informee is required if informing
is to take place. Again, this conclusion may be further supported
by appeal to the consistency and inconsistency tests.

I first apply the inconsistency test and consider the examples
below (again, I include examples which do not employ 'inform'
to contrast with those that do):

> The doctor informed John that he needed the operation, but John
> did not believe that he needed the operation.

> # The doctor convinced John that he needed the operation, but John
> did not believe that he needed the operation.

> Mary informed John that not everyone admired his work, but
> John believed that everyone admired his work.

> # Mary persuaded John that not everyone admired his work, but
> John believed that everyone admired his work.

There is no contradiction, no "felt inconsistency," in the examples in which it is claimed that an informee fails to believe
that of which he or she is informed. In this respect, 'inform'

contrasts with 'convince' and 'persuade', which do cause a felt inconsistency when used in sentences that juxtapose the claims that someone is convinced or persuaded that P with the claim that they fail to believe that P. Thus, the evidence of the inconsistency test is that sentences of the form 'X informs Y that P' do not entail those of the form 'Y believes that P'.

The same conclusion is supported by the consistency test, as the following examples illustrate:

? Mary convinced Janice that she was being obnoxious and Janice believed that she was being obnoxious.

Mary informed Janice that she was being obnoxious and Janice believed that she was being obnoxious.

? The defendant persuaded the jury that he was innocent, and the jury believed that the defendant was innocent.

The defendant informed the jury that he was innocent, and the jury believed that the defendant was innocent.

The first and third examples exhibit a performance oddity; one feels that the word 'and' should be replaced by the words 'and so' or 'and therefore', to make these sentences right. But this is not so for the second and fourth examples, which employ the verb 'inform'. Therefore, by the consistency test, informing someone that P does not require that they believe that P.

All the evidence presented in this section supports the conclusion that belief on the part of the informee is not required for informing to take place. Hence the answer to the second question listed above is that it is *not* the case that sentences of the form 'X informs Y that P' entail the corresponding belief sentences 'Y believes that P'.

7.3 CONCLUSION

Given the conclusions of the preceding two sections, it is obvious that, contrary to what we may have initially suspected, belief is not essentially involved in the process of informing. This is not to say that in general informants do not believe what they say, and informees do not believe what they are told, when informing takes place. Clearly belief usually is involved in instances of informing (which is why the discovery that believing is not essentially involved is important).

The reader should be reminded that although misinforming has not been explicitly considered in this chapter, our conclusions apply to misinforming as well as to informing. For, as noted in Chapter 5, 'inform' and 'misinform' behave alike in all respects except for their relationship to truth (as we saw in Chapter 6). With respect to the arguments and conclusions of this chapter, the reader may confirm that they readily translate into parallel arguments and conclusions regarding 'misinform'. Thus a further conclusion of this chapter is that belief is not required for misinforming to take place, or more precisely, that sentences of the form 'X misinforms Y that P' do not entail the corresponding belief sentences 'X believes that P' or 'Y believes that P'.

8
INFORMING, TELLING, AND KNOWING

Let us review the findings of the last three chapters regarding the necessary and sufficient conditions determining whether it is the case that X informs Y that P. In Chapter 5, we found that X informs Y that P only if Y receives and understands a message expressing the proposition that P, that is, only if X tells Y that P. In Chapter 6, we saw that it need not be the case that P for X to inform Y that P; in Chapter 7, we discovered that neither X nor Y must believe, or come to believe, that P in order for X to inform Y that P. Thus the only necessary condition of informing that has been discovered so far is that the informee receive and understand an appropriate message.

Can it be that there are no further necessary conditions of informing, and that receiving and understanding a message expressing the proposition that P is the *sufficient* as well as a necessary condition of informing someone that P? If so, then the result of our investigation of informing is both disappointing and somewhat suspect. This point can be made most forcefully by comparing informing with telling. As was established in Chapter 5, the necessary and sufficient condition for its being the case that X tells Y that P is that Y receive and understand a message expressing the proposition that P. Thus, if receiving and understanding an appropriate message is necessary and sufficient for informing, then informing and telling are the same process, that is, X informs Y that P if X tells Y that P. This does not seem correct. One's inclination is to insist that there is more to informing than just telling, that informing is a special sort of telling. In this chapter I take up the search for a further necessary condition of informing under the assumption that this inclination is correct, and that there indeed is more to informing than just telling.

The next section investigates the possibility that informing only takes place when the informant is reliable. The second section of the chapter investigates whether an informant must be in a position to know that P in order to inform another that P. The last section of the chapter summarizes the findings of Chapters 5 through 8 about informing and misinforming and consolidates them into analyses of 'inform' and 'misinform'.

8.1 INFORMING AND THE RELIABILITY OF THE INFORMANT

Informing plays a role in learning or coming to know; one way that Y comes to know that P is through having X inform Y that P. However, Y cannot come to *know* that P in this way unless being told that P by X constitutes adequate grounds for believing that P. In other words, X must be a *reliable informant* if Y is to learn that P from X. (I leave the notion of a "reliable informant" unanalyzed, for its detailed consideration would lead too far into epistemological considerations only tangentially related to our topic.)

On the other hand, recall from Chapter 5 that X may tell Y that p without it being the case that X is reliable. Thus perhaps it is the reliability of the informant which distinguishes informing from telling—but only if informing really does require that the informant be reliable. Hence this section addresses itself to the question of whether informing only occurs when the informant is reliable. In line with past practice, we may phrase this question more formally as follows:

> Do sentences of the form 'X informs Y that P' entail the corresponding sentences of the form 'X is a reliable informant concerning p'?

I argue that the entailment in question does not obtain. In support of this position, I offer a counter-example and evidence supplied by the consistency and inconsistency tests.

My counter-example involves Jones, a pathological liar, and Smith, a cat owner. Since Jones is a liar, much of what he says is untrue, though not everything that he says is untrue. Hence Jones is completely unreliable as an informant about anything. Suppose that Smith is aware of this, and consequently is inclined to be skeptical about anything that Jones claims to be the case. Now imagine that Jones witnesses the demise of Smith's cat at the wheels of a speeding truck, then rushes to Smith and tells him that his cat has been run over. Smith ignores Jones' claim, even though Jones insists that this time he is telling the truth and Smith's cat really has been run over.

Does Jones inform Smith that his cat has been run over? I submit that he does. Despite the fact that Jones is unreliable, as a matter of fact Jones *has* observed Smith's cat being run over, and *does* deliver an accurate report to Smith—Jones does inform Smith that his cat has been hit, although Smith (understandably) won't believe it. Though intuitions may differ regarding this case, it is clear to me that informing takes place in this example even though the informant is unreliable, and therefore that informing does not require that the informant be reliable.

Other counter-examples along these lines (the "boy-who-cried-wolf" lines) are easily generated, but they are no more (though no less) convincing than the one above. However appeal may be made, as usual, to the consistency and inconsistency tests for further evidence about the entailment under investigation.

With regard to the consistency test, consider the following examples (as usual, other examples are included for contrast):

John informed Mary that her car needed attention, and John is generally reliable about that sort of thing.

?Mary knew from John that her car needed attention, and John is generally reliable about that sort of thing.

Secretary Jones informed the media that new budget cuts are in the offing, and Jones is a reliable informant.

? The media learned from Secretary Jones that new budget cuts are in the offing, and Jones is a reliable informant.

The second and fourth sentences exhibit *very* slight performance oddities, explained by the fact that if one knows or learns from X that P, then X *must* be reliable; otherwise one could not really know or have learned that P. The first and third sentences, however, exhibit not even the slightest performance oddities. Hence the evidence from the consistency test agrees with the evidence provided by the counter-example in supporting the conclusion that informing does not require that the informant be reliable.

Now consider some examples generated for use in the inconsistency test:

John informed Mary that the professor had not announced a test in her absence, but John is not a reliable informant about that sort of thing.

Mary knew from John that the professor had not announced a test in her absence, but John is not a reliable informant about that sort of thing.

The Press-Secretary informed the media that no decision had been made, but the Press-Secretary is not particularly reliable.

The media learned from the Press-Secretary that no decision had been made, but the Press-Secretary is not particularly reliable.

The second sentence prompts one to wonder how Mary could *know* something from John if John is not a reliable informant, and the fourth sentence makes one wonder how the media could *learn* something from the Press-Secretary if the Press-Secretary is not particularly reliable. There is a very slight inconsistency felt with respect to the second and fourth sentences. However, there is no felt inconsistency whatever about the first and third sentences. According to the inconsistency test, then, sentences of the form 'X informs Y that P' do not entail those of the form 'X is a reliable informant concerning p', so informing does not require that the informant be reliable.

All the evidence supports the conclusion that having a reliable informant is not a necessary condition of informing. Given this conclusion, we have still not succeeded in pinpointing a feature of informing that distinguishes it from telling.

Before going on to the next section and the question of whether an informant must be in a position to know that P in order to inform someone that P, I should remark on the failing efficacy of the consistency and inconsistency tests. When these tests were first used in Chapter 6, they gave strong results because the examples that were considered so clearly exhibited performance oddities or inconsistencies. For example, it is obvious to any native speaker that

? It's unfortunate that the Pope was shot, and the Pope was shot.

is rather odd, and that the sentence

John knew that Fran did it, but Fran did not do it.

is inconsistent. The clarity of the examples decreased somewhat in Chapter 7. Although it is still quite undeniable that the sentence

? John knows that Fran did it and John believes that Fran did it.

exhibits a performance oddity, while the sentence

John is certain that it cost twenty dollars but John doesn't believe that it cost twenty dollars.

feels inconsistent, there is a decrease in the force of one's linguistic intuitions regarding these latter examples in comparison to the former. Nevertheless, one's intuitions are still quite robust.

The examples exhibited in this section, however, barely arouse feelings of inconsistency or oddness, despite the fact that they should do so given the entailment relations involved. For example, it seems clear that one can know or learn that P only if one has adequate grounds for believing that P.[†] In particular, if

---

[†] See (Lehrer 1974) for a typical discussion of the need for adequate grounds for believing that P in knowing that P.

one knows or learns something from some person X, then the fact that X supplies the information must be adequate grounds for believing that P—in other words, X must be a reliable informant with respect to p. Therefore knowing or learning that P from an informant requires that the informant be reliable, and sentences of the form 'Y knows (learns) from X that P' entail sentences of the form 'X is a reliable informant about p'. Given these facts, one would expect that the examples employing 'know' and 'learn' above would exhibit clear performance oddities and inconsistencies, respectively. But this is not so. The examples are only the slightest bit odd or inconsistent.

How is this phenomenon to be explained? I believe that it may be explained by the fact that the consistency and inconsistency tests rely completely on our linguistic intuitions regarding the legitimate use of *ordinary* language. Consequently, they cannot be relied upon to produce results in cases where technical terminology or jargon is employed. Hence, the consistency and inconsistency tests do not produce very strong results when used on sentences like those above because they employ the rather technical phrase 'being a reliable informant'.

This fact can be brought out quite forcefully by considering an entailment between sentences employing terms of a purely technical nature. For example, an important result in formal language theory is that every context-free language is accepted by a push-down automaton (PDA). Hence it is true that the sentence 'Algol is a context-free language' entails 'Algol is accepted by a PDA'. But consider the following conjunctions with the consistency and inconsistency tests in mind:

Algol is a context-free language and Algol is accepted by a PDA.

Algol is a context-free language but Algol is not accepted by a PDA.

Given the entailment mentioned above, the first of these sentences is redundant, while the second is inconsistent. Yet neither of them arouse any objection whatever based on *linguistic* intuitions. Specifically, the first does not exhibit a performance oddity and the second is not felt to be inconsistent. Even someone aware of the fact that every context-free language is accepted by a PDA does not object to these sentences on linguistic grounds; no rule of ordinary language establishes that any entailments obtain between the sentences involved.

We must expect, then, that when considering entailments involving sentences employing a good deal of technical terminology, the consistency and inconsistency tests will prove quite useless. Unfortunately, this is likely to occur quite soon; in the next section we take up the question of whether informing someone that P requires that the informant be in a position to know that P. The latter phrase is technical enough to make it likely that the difficulties encountered in this section with the consistency and inconsistency tests will recur.

8.2 INFORMING AND BEING IN A POSITION TO KNOW

Despite having considered a wide range of phenomena involved in communication, we have still not succeeded in discovering any feature of informing that distinguishes it from telling. In continuing to look for such a distinguishing feature, it may help to compare the sorts of situations that people typically describe using the term 'inform' with those that are typically described using 'tell'.

It should be noted in passing that 'inform' is a performative verb. Though interesting, this feature of 'inform' is not very important for our purposes, so the fact has not been stressed. Particularly with respect to the question at hand, 'tell' is also a performative verb, so being a performative verb does not distinguish 'inform' and 'tell'. See Austin (1975) for the definitive discussion of performatives.

To begin with, 'tell' is clearly a much less formal term than is 'inform'. We use 'tell' to talk about everyday discourse and communication, with 'inform' generally being reserved for more ritualistic and important sorts of communication. Thus, we are more inclined to say that John *told* Mary that he wasn't in the mood for pizza than we are to say that John *informed* Mary that he wasn't in the mood for pizza. In contrast, when Jones the policeman makes an arrest, he *informs* the suspect of his rights, not *tells* him of his rights, and when Smith the Press-Secretary makes an announcement to the press, we typically say that Smith *informs* the press, not *tells* the press, that such and such is the case.

In general, then, we use 'inform' to refer to instances in which some figure of authority tells someone something (usually something important). But note that not *every* authority counts, even when something important is said. One is not inclined to say that Jones the policeman *informs* his friend Scott that he should invest in money market certificates, but that Jones *told* Scott that he should do this; and likewise one describes Press-Secretary Smith as having *told*, not *informed*, a reporter that he should see a specialist about his back problem. We use 'inform' to describe cases in which an *epistemic authority* regarding p tells someone that P, not just any authority. A policeman is an epistemic authority about the rights of arrestees but not (generally) about the investment market. Hence policemen inform arrestees of their rights but tell their friends about investments. A Press-Secretary is an epistemic authority about the activities of an administration, but not (generally) about health problems. Thus a Press-Secretary is said to inform reporters about budget cuts but to tell reporters what they should do about their health problems.

The characteristic feature of an epistemic authority (concerning p) is that an epistemic authority is in *a position to know that P*. Could it be that informing someone that P generally requires that the informant be in a position to know that P? This question is the focus of our discussion in this section.

8.2.1 Being in a Position to Know

Although I intend to leave the notion of "being in a position to know" as a primitive (i.e., unanalyzed) notion, there is still much to be said, short of a complete analysis, regarding what is meant by it. First, although I have used, and will continue to use, the locution 'being in a position to know *that* P', this should be understood in the sense of 'being in a position to know whether p is true or not'. In other words, there is no imputation of the truth of p in my use of the former phrase, just as there is none in the latter. Hence being in a position to know that P is just the same as being in a position to know that not-P, and both are the same as being in a position to know whether p is the case.

Being in a position to know that P is distinct from both knowing that P and believing that P. This can be illustrated with an example. Suppose that Jones glances at an accurate thermometer to find out what the temperature is, and she thinks that she sees that it reads seventy degrees. In fact, however, Jones has misread the thermometer, and it actually indicates that the temperature is seventy-two degrees. Now, because Jones has consulted a thermometer registering the correct temperature, and Jones has formulated the belief that it is seventy degrees on this basis, Jones is in a position to know that it is seventy degrees. But since it is really seventy-two degrees, and her belief is false, Jones does not *know* that it is seventy degrees.

Likewise, because Jones has consulted a thermometer which accurately registers the temperature, Jones is in a position to know that the temperature is seventy-two degrees. However, because of her mistake, Jones does not believe that the temperature is seventy-two degrees. Hence Jones neither believes nor knows (since knowing entails believing) that the temperature is seventy-two degrees, although Jones is in a position to know this.

Of course, knowing that P entails that the knower is in a position to know that P. One cannot learn that P by magic; one must be justified in believing that P, which is what being in a position to know amounts to. (Readers skeptical of this claim should note the examples employing 'know' and 'being in a position to know' a few pages hence, which clearly indicate, via the consistency and inconsistency tests, that knowing entails being in a position to know.)

Being in a position to know that P is also different from being in a position to *find out* that P. I may be able to go to the library to look up the atomic weight of lithium, so I am in a position to *find out* the atomic weight of lithium. However, I am not in a position to *know* the atomic weight of lithium, for I have no evidence whatever on this score. Once I go to the library, *then* I will be in a position to know this fact, but not until then. Being in a position to know that P involves apparently *having* adequate justification for the belief that P, not being in a position to *obtain* adequate justification for the belief that P.

In summary, then, being in a position to know that P involves apparently having adequate justification to support a belief concerning whether p is the case. It does not require believing or knowing that P, although knowing that P entails that the knower is in a position to know that P.

8.2.2 A Necessary Condition of Informing and Misinforming

Having somewhat clarified what being in a position to know amounts to, we are ready to consider arguments to the effect that informing someone that P can only take place when the informant is in a position to know that P, or in other words, the claim that

> Sentences of the form 'X informs Y that P' entail sentences of the form 'X is in a position to know that P.'

We begin our consideration of this claim by considering a case in which an alleged informant is not in a position to know.

Suppose that Jones, a shyster, has set himself up as an art appraiser. In fact Jones knows absolutely nothing about art and has no basis at all for any of his "appraisals." Now suppose that Smith presents Jones with a painting, asking for an appraisal. Jones tells Smith that his painting is worth $5000. Is it correct to say that Jones *informs* Smith of the worth of his painting? It seems not. This is so even if, by chance, Smith's painting really *is* worth $5000. For even if Jones guesses the worth of Smith's painting, the fact that Jones has no basis whatever for his statement seems to preclude the possibility that Jones can inform Smith about its worth. I suggest, then, that since Jones is not in a position to know the worth of Smith's painting, Jones cannot inform Smith that it is worth $5000.

This example seems to indicate that informing requires being in a position to know; we now need further evidence in order to establish this position firmly. As discussed in Chapter 6, the way to provide evidence in favor of claims to the effect that an entailment obtains (besides considering various examples) is to apply the consistency and inconsistency tests. However, as remarked in the last section, the consistency and inconsistency tests are not efficacious regarding entailments involving technical terminology. Unfortunately, the entailment presently under consideration involves a technical phrase (viz., 'being in a position to know'). Hence we may expect that direct application of the consistency and inconsistency tests will be rather fruitless. Nevertheless, we will apply these tests and see how they fare.

Consider the following examples generated in accord with the consistency test:

> John informed Mary that her oil was low, and John was in a position to know.

> John told Mary that her oil was low, and John was in a position to know.

> ? John knew that Mary's oil was low, and John was in a position to know.

I find that the first sentence exhibits a performance oddity, but it is so slight that I hesitate to count it as anything but wishful thinking. The second is clearly acceptable and the last clearly odd. According to the consistency test, the third sentence should be odd, but so should the first, if informing really does require being in a position to know. Since it is not, we must choose between two conclusions: either the thesis that informing requires that the informant be in a position to know is wrong, or the entailment under examination involves too technical a phrase to be detected by the consistency test. Since there is not a good way to choose between these alternatives, it seems best to regard the consistency test as having failed to provide any good evidence whatever about the claim under examination.

Turning to the inconsistency test, we consider the following examples:

> Mary informed John that the mail had arrived, but she was not in a position to know this.

Mary told John that the mail had arrived, but she was not in a position to know this.

Mary knew that the mail had arrived, but she was not in a position to know this.

According to the inconsistency test, there should be no felt inconsistency regarding the second sentence, but felt inconsistency regarding the third; this is the case. In addition, there should be felt inconsistency regarding the first sentence providing that informing requires being in a position to know. Although I detect a very slight inconsistency regarding the first sentence, my intuitions are not strong enough to serve as the basis for any strong claims in this regard. But again, this may be due to the "non-ordinary language" nature of the phrase 'being in a position to know', rather than due to the failure of the entailment. So, once again, the best course is to regard the inconsistency test as having failed to provide evidence of value in determining whether the claim under examination is correct.

Fortunately, a bit of ingenuity enables us to yet derive some evidence from the inconsistency test. Since part of the difficulty in effectively applying the inconsistency test arises from the technical flavor of the phrase 'being in a position to know', the test may be more successful if we can use it on sentences containing more ordinary terminology. Suppose that S is such a sentence. Furthermore, suppose that S is inconsistent with the sentence

Q. X is in a position to know that P.

Then, if the sentence

R. X informs Y that P.

really does entail Q, it must be the case that S is also inconsistent with R. Provided that the inconsistency of R and S is sufficiently obvious, the conjunction of R and S ought to produce a feeling of inconsistency. In short, if informing really does require being in a position to know, then the conjunction of R and S (where

S is inconsistent with Q), should produce feelings of inconsistency. Hence such a response would constitute evidence in favor of our hypothesis.

We must now find sentences to stand in place of S in this argument. Such sentences must contain ordinary terminology so as to pique our intuitions about ordinary language, yet be inconsistent with sentence Q above. I suggest that the following forms of sentences fit this bill:

X is only guessing that P.

X only has a hunch that P.

There is no way for X to know that P.

X has no evidence for the hypothesis that P.

In support of the claim that these are inconsistent with X's being in a position to know that P, recall the characterization of being in a position to know as apparently being justified with respect to a belief regarding p. If X is only guessing that P, or only has a hunch that P, then certainly X is *not* justified in a belief that P obtains. Likewise, if X has no evidence for the hypothesis that P, then X has no justification for any hypothesis regarding p. Finally, if there is not a way for X to know that P, then X can hardly be in a position to know that P. Hence the inconsistency of the above sentences with X's being in a position to know that P is pretty obvious.

We now need only demonstrate that sentences in which p and one of the four kinds of sentences discussed in the last paragraph are conjoined feel inconsistent. To this end, consider the following sentences:

Bob informed me that Mary was angry, but Bob was only guessing that she was angry.

Bob told me that Mary was angry, but Bob was only guessing that she was angry.

LeStrade informed Holmes that the butler did it, but it was only a hunch.

LeStrade told Holmes that the butler did it, but it was only a hunch.

Professor Smith informed his class that Socrates was diabetic, but there is no way he could have known this.

Professor Smith told his class that Socrates was diabetic, but there is no way he could have known this.

John informed me that Kennedy had been killed in a conspiracy, but admitted he had no evidence for his claim.

John told me that Kennedy had been killed in a conspiracy, but admitted he had no evidence for his claim.

The sentences employing 'inform' all feel somewhat inconsistent, particularly when contrasted with the sentences employing 'tell'. Thus we have evidence to support the claim that being in a position to know that P is a necessary condition for being able to inform someone that p.

I conclude that informing does, after all, differ in a significant respect from telling. X may tell Y that P simply by saying that P to Y in such a way that Y understands that X is claiming that P. However, in order to inform Y that P, X must not only tell Y that P, X must also be in a position to know that P. Thus, informing is a special sort of telling; it is the sort of telling that takes place when an epistemic authority on p issues a judgment regarding p.

As in previous chapters, this conclusion is extended to include misinforming as well. Specifically, I conclude that

Sentences of the form 'X misinforms Y that P' entail sentences of the form 'X is in a position to know that P'.

The arguments employed above to establish our conclusion regarding 'inform' may be converted into arguments in support of this conclusion about 'misinform' by simply substituting the latter term for the former.

8.3 ANALYSES OF 'INFORM' AND 'MISINFORM'

We have now completed our investigation of the processes of informing and misinforming. The purpose of the present section is to consolidate our findings into analyses of 'inform' and 'misinform', and to summarize the other major results generated in the course of the last four chapters.

In Chapter 5 it was determined that informing and misinforming are species of telling. In this chapter a further necessary condition of informing and misinforming someone that P has been uncovered, namely that an informant must be in a position to know that P. Finally, in Chapter 6 it was discovered that misinforming requires falsity, though informing does not require truth. Assuming that no further necessary conditions have escaped our attention, the analyses of 'inform' and 'misinform' resulting from our investigation are the following:

X *informs* Y that P if
  1. X tells Y that P,
  2. X is in a position to know that P.
X *misinforms* Y that P if
  1. X tells Y that P,
  2. X is in a position to know that P,
  3. p is false.

In view of the analysis of telling propounded in Chapter 5, both of these analyses may be restated as follows:

X *informs* Y that P if
  1. there exists a set $ of sentences such that
    (a) X sends $ to Y in context i,
    (b) Y receives and understands the sentences of $,
    (c) p is the conglomerate proposition expressed by $ in context i,
  2. X is in a position to know that P.
X *misinforms* Y that P if
  1. there exists a set $ of sentences such that
    (a) X sends $ to Y in context i,
    (b) Y receives and understands the sentences of $,
    (c) p is the conglomerate proposition expressed by $, in context i,

2. X is in a position to know that P,
3. p is false.

Finally, given these analyses, it is clear that we can characterize misinforming in terms of informing as follows:

X *misinforms* Y that P if
 1. X informs Y that P,
 2. p is false.

Although the above analyses are the main results of the last four chapters, there are a number of minor conclusions that nonetheless deserve to be summarized. First, in Chapter 5, it was argued that if X tells Y that P, then X says to Y that P, though not conversely. Hence every case of informing someone that P is a case of saying to them that P, but not conversely.

In Chapter 6, many interesting conclusions about sentence-complementing terms were established. Specifically with respect to 'inform' and 'misinform', it turns out that 'inform' is a non-factive non-assertive sentence-complementing term. Consequently sentences that employ 'inform' as their main verb neither presuppose, nor entail without presupposing, their complement sentences. In this respect, 'inform' is like 'tell', 'say', 'assert', 'conjecture', and a host of other non-factive non-assertive sentence-complementing terms.

In contrast, 'misinform' is a counter-assertive sentence-complementing term; sentences employing 'misinform' as their main verb entail the negation of their complement sentences. Other counter-assertive terms are 'lie', 'incorrect', 'mistaken', and 'false'.

Chapters 7 and 8 provide several conclusions regarding the *lack* of any systematic connection between informing and several other notions. These conclusions are important because it is so commonly believed that such connections do obtain. In particular, it seems to be a commonly held opinion that informing and misinforming are systematically related to believing. However, this is not so. It need not be the case that X or Y believe, or come to believe, that P in order that X inform Y that P, as is shown in Chapter 7. In Chapter 8, on the other hand, it is argued that an informant need not be reliable in order to inform someone that P.

These conclusions will be made use of very soon, for in the next chapter I will argue that most of them can be extended to conclusions about information and misinformation. Hence the work of the preceding four chapters will contribute significantly to the task of analyzing 'information' and 'misinformation'.

9
INFORMING AND INFORMATION

We have been concerned in the last four chapters to investigate the processes of informing and misinforming. This investigation culminated in the analyses of 'inform' and 'misinform' presented at the end of the last chapter. In the present chapter, we take up the thread of the discussion of information broken off at the end of Chapter 4 by extending our discoveries about informing and misinforming into conclusions about information and misinformation. The first section of this chapter lays the groundwork for this extension by formulating and defending principles linking informing and information, and misinforming and misinformation. Subsequent sections make use of these principles, along with our results about the nature of informing and misinforming, to establish theses about the relationships between information, misinformation, and truth, information and belief, and information and being in a position to know. These results are then combined with the results from Chapter 4 about the propositional analysis of information to produce final versions of the propositional analysis, and of analyses of the notions of containing, transferring, and conveying information. The last section of the chapter concludes the study.

9.1 THE LINKING PRINCIPLE

Epistemology is also known as the theory of knowledge, and most epistemologists would agree that one of the questions they

try to answer is "What is knowledge?" Epistemological investigation, however, usually focuses not on the noun 'knowledge'
but on the verb 'to know'. Once a position regarding 'know' is
established, it is then extended into a position regarding 'knowledge'. Usually this extension is made on the basis of an implicit
appeal to some principle connecting knowledge and knowing.
Since such principles are implicit, it is difficult to know exactly
what they are; presumably, however, they are truisms such as
"knowledge is that which is known." But whatever the operative
principles, it is still the case that the usual *modus operandi* in
epistemological investigation is to concentrate on analyzing
knowing and then to extend the results of the analysis into
conclusions about knowledge.

There are several good reasons for this practice. First, the
requirement that our theories be systematic and coherent (see
section 1.2.5) demands that the analyses of cognate terms such
as 'know' and 'knowledge' fit tightly together. Certainly any
position that drives a wedge between knowledge and knowing
would be *prima facie* suspect. Hence one expects conclusions
about 'know' to be extensible to conclusions about 'knowledge'.

There are also certain practical advantages to this approach.
Focusing attention on knowing tends to make the difficult ontological questions that arise in the analysis of knowledge less
pressing. Second, and more importantly, for some reason it seems
to make the task of teasing out some of the subtle factors involved
in having knowledge a little easier. Since this task is extremely
difficult under any circumstances, anything we can do to make
it easier is worth doing.

Of course, not every question involved in the analysis of
'knowledge' is answered by an analysis of 'know'; in particular,
ontological questions about the nature of knowledge may not
be answered by an analysis of 'know'. Nevertheless, an analysis
of 'know' supplies many important facts of use in developing
an analysis of 'knowledge'. For example, suppose that knowing
is analyzed as a relation between a person X and a proposition
p such that the following holds:

X knows that P if
   (i) p is true,
   (ii) X believes that P,
   (iii) X is justified in believing that P.

Ignoring the question of whether this analysis is correct, we can still consider some of the consequences it has for an analysis of 'knowledge'. Suppose we appeal to the principle that knowledge is that which is known. Then we may conclude that knowledge requires truth. Furthermore, it follows that knowledge is somehow essentially involved with belief—perhaps knowledge is a sort of belief, or is sets of beliefs of some believer or community of believers. Finally, we may conclude that knowledge (whatever it is) must be justified. Thus an investigation of the nature of knowledge can profit significantly from the results of an investigation of knowing.

The words 'inform' and 'information' are related to one another much as are the words 'know' and 'knowledge', and many of the remarks made above concerning the latter pair are true also of the former. If requirements of systematicity and coherence demand coordination between the analyses of 'know' and 'knowledge', so also do they demand coordination between the analyses of 'inform' and 'information'. Hence we may expect to be justified in extending many of our conclusions about 'inform' to conclusions about 'information'. Furthermore, the discoveries we've made about informing can be put to good use in carrying out an analysis of the nature of information. For we have reached conclusions about the connections between informing and several other things (like truth, belief, and being in a position to know) that are not yet matched by any of our conclusions about information. Hence I propose to emulate the epistemologists in their practice of extending conclusions about 'know' to conclusions about 'knowledge' by extending many of our conclusions about 'inform' to conclusions about 'information'.

In order to carry out this task, we need some general principle connecting 'inform' with 'information' to parallel the principle connecting 'know' and 'knowledge' that the epistemologists (implicitly) appeal to. In formulating such a principle, the main considerations seem to be the following:

1. The principle should demonstrate a systematic connection between 'inform' and 'information.'
2. The principle should be as unobjectionable as possible.

The first requirement is merely an explicit statement for the case at hand of the general requirement that analyses be coherent and systematic. The second requirement arises from the fact that the principle in question will be employed as an important premise in several arguments in which conclusions about information will be drawn on the basis of evidence about informing. Such arguments will be defensible only if the principle by virtue of which results about informing are extended to conclusions about information is quite unassailable. Hence this principle should be as weak as possible; ideally it should appear trivial or obvious.

Above I suggested that epistemologists implicitly appeal to some sort of truism like "knowledge is that which is known" in moving from conclusions about knowing to conclusions about knowledge. Such a principle is both obvious and demonstrates a systematic connection between knowing and knowledge. On the model of this epistemological claim, I frame the following assertion regarding the connection between informing and information:

Information is that which is conveyed when X informs Y that P.

Only a few moments' consideration prompt one to assent to this claim as obvious. For suppose that X informs Y that P. What is passed from X to Y in this process? Obviously, the information that P. Hence I suggest that this commonplace is completely unobjectionable.

In order that this principle serve as a bridge between informing and information in our discussion, it must be made somewhat more precise and formal. Consequently I frame the following principle, which I will call the *Linking Principle* (LP), based on the truism introduced above:

LP: X informs Y that P if X passes the information that P to Y.

This principle, I believe, satisfies both of the requirements listed above. First, it clearly asserts a close systematic relationship between informing and information; it asserts, in fact, necessary and sufficient conditions for informing in terms of information. Second, it is (I hope) quite unobjectionable, being no more than a more precise articulation of the truism cited above.

So far in this section I have mentioned only information, informing, and a principle linking the two. Misinformation and misinforming must of course likewise be linked. Hence we formulate the *Complementary Linking Principle* (CLP) for misinformation and misinforming:

CLP: X misinforms Y that P if X passes the misinformation that P to Y.

Again I claim that the CLP, like the LP, satisfies requirements 1 and 2 enumerated above.

9.2 INFORMATION, MISINFORMATION, AND TRUTH

In this section results about the connection between informing, misinforming, and truth are extended via the LP and the CLP to conclusions about the connection between information, misinformation, and truth. Further support for these conclusions is obtained by applying the consistency and inconsistency tests.

In Chapter 6 it was established that informing does not require truth; even if p is not true, it may still be the case that someone may inform another that P. In line with this finding, suppose that X, Y, and P are such that X informs Y that P, but P is false. According to the LP, if X informs Y that P then X passes the information that P to Y. But it is false that P. Hence the information that P is false. Therefore, information may be false.

The results of applying the consistency and inconsistency tests support this conclusion. Regarding the former, if information need not be true, then there should be no performance oddity in tacking the assertion that P onto the end of an assertion that P is information, and otherwise such a claim should exhibit a performance oddity. Consider the following examples:

He sent John the information that Rodney would default and Rodney did default.

The letter contains the information that John's project is nearly complete and it's true that John's project is nearly complete.

These sentences are not odd at all. Hence the consistency test supports our conclusion.

Now consider the following sentences generated to test for felt inconsistency between the claim that P is information and the claim that P is false:

> He sent John the information that Rodney would default but Rodney didn't default.

> The CIA Director is accused of having provided false and misleading information to the Senate committee.

> The information in that cable must be false!

These sentences are not at all inconsistent, as they would be if information could not be false. Thus the consistency and inconsistency tests provide evidence in agreement with the conclusion derived from the analysis of informing by way of the LP. Consequently I adopt the position that information may be false.

In contrast, we may use the CLP to establish that misinformation *must* be false. For suppose to the contrary that misinformation need not be false. Let the misinformation that P be true, and suppose that X passes the misinformation that P to Y. Then, according to the CLP, X misinforms Y that P. But, given our discovery that misinforming requires falsity, it follows that P is false, a contradiction. Hence our initial assumption is reduced to absurdity, so misinformation must be false.

Let us now use the consistency test to try this conclusion. Consider the following:

> ?The misinformation in your statement is quite false.

> The allegation in your statement is quite false.

> ?His article contains the misinformation that Goldbach's conjecture is proven, but it's false that Goldbach's conjecture is proven.

> His article contains the statement that Goldbach's conjecture is proven, but it's false that Goldbach's conjecture is proven.

> ?The misinformation in that cable is false.

The sentences employing 'misinformation' exhibit a performance oddity, which is made especially noticeable when they are contrasted with similar sentences that do not employ this term. Hence the verdict of the consistency test is that misinformation must be false.

The same verdict is returned by the inconsistency test, as the following sentences illustrate:

\# His letter contained the misinformation that John had broken his arm, and John had broken his arm.

His letter contained the speculation that John had broken his arm, and John had broken his arm.

\# The misinformation in that cable is true.

\# Rather gave the nation the misinformation that Smith was dead, and Smith was dead.

Rather gave the nation the report that Smith was dead, and Smith was dead.

The sentences employing 'misinformation' are clearly inconsistent, which supports the claim that misinformation must be false.

All the evidence is in favor of the thesis that misinformation must be false. Since information may be false, we see that misinformation is a species of information, just as misinforming is a species of informing. Thus a coherent picture of the relationships between informing, information, misinforming, misinformation, and truth has emerged: informing does not require truth, and information need not be true; but misinforming requires falsehood, and misinformation must be false.

9.3 INFORMATION AND BELIEF

We next turn to consideration of the connection between information and belief. Once again, the main argument proceeds by extending results about informing to conclusions about information via the LP, but the consistency and inconsistency test will also be employed in a supporting role.

Recall that in Chapter 7 it was discovered that neither belief on the part of an informant, nor on the part of an informee, are required for informing to take place. Thus it may be the case, for example, that neither X nor Y believe that P, but nevertheless that X informs Y that P. In fact, we may suppose that no one believes that P at all—even so, it still may be that X informs Y that P. In such cases, according to the LP, it follows that X passes the information that P to Y. Hence it may be that the information that P is believed by no one. Therefore, information need not be believed in order to be information.

A quick application of the consistency and inconsistency tests verifies this conclusion. According to the consistency test, if information must be believed by someone, then the following sentences should exhibit a performance oddity:

> The professor passed along the information, and someone believed it.

> The General shared his information that the Russians have a particle-beam weapon with the committee, and they believed it.

These sentences do not exhibit performance oddities, in support of our conclusion.

Now consider the following examples generated in accord with the inconsistency test:

> The spacecraft had the information that the atmosphere was fifty percent nitrogen, but no one believed it.

> The professor passed along the information, but no one believed it, not even him.

> I'm sure no one believes the information in that cable!

These sentences are not inconsistent at all. The inconsistency test therefore also provides evidence endorsing our conclusion.

It is clear from the arguments in this section that information need not be believed by anyone in order to be information. There is, then, no systematic relation between information and belief, and belief need not enter into the analysis of information *per se*. (Of course, belief is an essential part of the notion of the information conveyed by a sentence; this point is taken up again below.) This does not mean, however, that in general information is not believed by anyone; clearly we all believe a lot of information. It simply means that it isn't necessary for anyone to believe that P in order that P be information.

Finally, the reader is reminded that a parallel discussion is easily constructed to show that misinformation need not be believed by anyone either. The details of such a discussion are left to the reader.

9.4 INFORMATION AND BEING IN A POSITION TO KNOW

In this section we undertake to extend our finding that X must be in a position to know that P in order to inform anyone that P into a parallel conclusion regarding information. Although difficulties are to be expected with regard to using the consistency and inconsistency tests to verify this conclusion (on account of the fact that it involves the technical phrase 'being in a position to know'—see section 8.2 for discussion of this point), we will nevertheless attempt to use these tests to add evidence in favor of the account.

Of necessity, any thesis connecting information with being in a position to know must be framed in terms of some individual who possesses, or receives, or sends, the information. For clearly there must be some entity that is the thing which is in a position to know—information itself certainly cannot be in a position to know anything. Hence our hypothesis in this section is that information is specially connected to some individual privileged to be in a position to know.

Let us use the LP to consider who this individual must be. Suppose that X informs Y that P. Then by the LP, X passes the information that P to Y. Regarding being in a position to know, recall from the last chapter that if X informs Y that P, then X must be in a position to know that P. Hence the information that P is passed from, or *originates* from, some individual X in a position to know that P. On this basis, I propose that

> The information that P must originate with some individual in a position to know that P.

(More will be said about the notion of information "originating" with some individual when we consider how to incorporate this conclusion into our analyses of containing, transferring, and conveying information in the next section of this chapter.)

The last paragraph uses the LP to motivate our hypothesis; we now employ the LP to argue in its favor. The argument proceeds by contradiction. Suppose that the hypothesis is false, that it need not be the case that the information that P originates from some individual in a position to know that P. Let X be an individual not in a position to know that P who nevertheless has the information that P, and passes it to some individual Y. Then by the LP, X informs Y that P. Since X informs Y that P only if X is in a position to know that P, it follows that X is in a position to know that P, a contradiction. Therefore the information that P must originate with some individual in a position to know that P.

Our next task is to attempt to provide independent evidence in support of this claim using the consistency and inconsistency tests. As in the parallel case for 'inform' (see section 8.2), these tests do not provide much evidence when used on sentences employing the phrase 'being in a position to know', but the inconsistency test does supply some support when used on sentences employing certain other terms.

First consider the following sentences as grist for the consistency test:

> Professor Smith published that information about stellar spectra, and Smith is in a position to know about stellar spectra.

> John came up with the information that Harry and Stella are having an affair, and John is in a position to know about it.

> The information that animals had gotten into the food originated with Mary, and she was in a position to know that they had.

All three of these sentences ought to exhibit a performance oddity if our thesis is correct.. However, they do not (or else the oddity is so slight as to be virtually unnoticeable). This result would constitute evidence against our position were it not for the demonstrated inadequacy of the consistency test when used on sentences employing technical terminology. Hence we should conclude that the consistency test here provides no reliable evidence either for or against our hypothesis.

Much the same occurs with the inconsistency test. Consider the following examples:

> Professor Smith published that information about stellar spectra, but Smith is not in a position to know about stellar spectra.

> John came up with the information that Harry and Stella are having an affair, though John is not in a position to know about it.

> The information that animals had gotten into the food originated with Mary, but Mary was not in a position to know that they had.

Again, all three of these sentences should feel inconsistent if being in a position to know is required of an originator of information, yet these sentences (except, perhaps, for the second) do not feel very inconsistent. As before, there are two candidates for the explanation of this result: either our hypothesis is false, or the inconsistency test is misleading in this case on account of the technical phrase 'being in a position to know' employed in the examples. Consequently we conclude that the inconsistency test provides no trustworthy evidence either for or against our account.

As suggested in section 8.2.2, we may yet be able to use the inconsistency test to generate some reliable evidence concerning the claim under consideration. For being in a position to know that P is apparently inconsistent with only guessing or having a hunch that P, with having no way of knowing that P, and with having no evidence for the hypothesis that P. Thus if the information that P must originate with someone in a position to know that P, it cannot originate with someone who is only guessing or only has a hunch that P, or who has no evidence or no way of knowing that P. Thus claims to the effect that the information that P originates with someone who is only guessing that P, or has a hunch that P, and so on, should feel inconsistent. With this method of operation in mind, consider the following examples:

Professor Jones published the information that Pluto has two moons, but he admits that he has no evidence that this is so.

Professor Jones published the claim that Pluto has two moons, but he admits that he has no evidence that this is so.

John came up with the information that Harry and Stella were having an affair, but confessed he was only guessing.

John came up with the story that Harry and Stella were having an affair, but confessed he was only guessing.

Bob is the source of the information that Mary has been having nightmares, but there is no way Bob could have known this.

Bob is the source of the rumor that Mary has been having nightmares, but there is no way Bob could have known this.

Jones originated the information that Secretary Smith had been indicted, but he only had a hunch that this was so.

Jones originated the report that Secretary Smith had been indicted, but he only had a hunch that this was so.

The sentences employing information feel inconsistent while those that do not are perfectly acceptable. According to the inconsistency test, this means that being in a position to know that P *is* required of the originator of the information that P.

It goes without saying, of course, that this conclusion is matched by another: the misinformation that P must likewise originate with someone in a position to know that P. As usual, we do not bother to rehearse arguments for this conclusion because they exactly parallel those presented above.

In summary, we have seen that the fact that an informant must be in a position to know has a consequence for information: information must originate with someone who is in a position to know. This conclusion is supported by an argument from the nature of informing and the LP and by independent evidence from the inconsistency test.

This completes the task of extending the results of the investigation of informing and misinforming in Chapters 5 through 8 into conclusions about the nature of information and misinformation. It remains to combine these conclusions about information and misinformation with the propositional analysis of information and misinformation stated in Chapter 4. This is carried out in the next section of this chapter.

9.5 EXTENDING THE PROPOSITIONAL ANALYSIS

The general statement of the propositional analysis of information from Chapter 4 is as follows:

> The *information* carried by a set $ of sentences is the proposition p, where p is the conglomerate proposition expressed by some set $' of sentences appropriately associated with $.

In Chapter 4 it was noted that this analysis (and the arguments presented in its development) neglects certain important problems about the nature of information. Among these unaddressed problems are (i) whether a proposition must be true to be information, (ii) whether a proposition must come to be believed by some individual to be information, and (iii) whether any conditions are required of the originator of information. Thanks to the discussion carried out since Chapter 4, we are now in a position to answer these questions, and to make any necessary changes in the propositional analysis required by the answers.

Regarding the first question, we found in section 9.2 that information need not be true. Hence a proposition need not be true in order to be information, and no emendation of the propositional analysis is required.

Likewise, the answer to the second question does not force any change in the propositional analysis. For in section 9.3 it was established that information need not be believed by anyone, including the informee, to be information. Thus it is not necessary that a proposition come to be believed by some individual to be information.

The third question mentioned above does force the introduction of complications in the propositional analysis. It is true, as demonstrated in section 9.3, that the originator of the information that P need not believe that P in order for p to be information. But, as shown in section 9.4, the originator of the information that P must be in a position to know that P. Hence the propositional analysis must be amended to take this discovery into account. Consequently, I introduce the following change in the analysis:

> The *information* carried by a set $ of sentences is the proposition p such that
> 1. p is the conglomerate proposition expressed by a set $' of sentences appropriately associated with $,
> 2. there exists an individual X, the originator of $, who is in a position to know that P.

Thus sentences carry the information that P provided that they express the proposition that P, and that they originate with someone in a position to know that P, regardless of whether p is true or whether anyone believes that P.

It is clear (as it was in Chapter 4) that this analysis prompts one to wonder about the phrase 'a set $' of sentences appropriately associated with $'. It also prompts one to wonder about what sort of individual counts as the 'originator of $.' Both of these issues are taken up in the three subsections below in which the notions of containing, transferring, and conveying information are reconsidered in light of the above emendation of the propositional analysis.

Before going on to these three notions, however, we should, for the sake of completeness, explicitly and formally state the propositional analysis of misinformation that goes along with our propositional analysis of information. The only difference between the two is that misinformation *must* be false. Adding this condition to the analysis of information above, we arrive at the following:

The *misinformation* carried by a set $ of sentences is the proposition
p such that
1. p is the conglomerate proposition expressed by a set $' of
   sentences appropriately associated with $,
2. there exists an individual X, the originator of $, who is in a
   position to know that P,
3. p is false.

As with the analysis of information stated above, it remains to
specify what is meant by the phrases 'a set $' of sentences ap-
propriately associated with $,' and 'the originator of $'.' The next
three subsections satisfy this need by reconsidering the notions
of the information contained in, transferred by, and conveyed
by, a set of sentences.

9.5.1 Information Contained

To begin our reconsideration of the notion of the information
contained in a set of sentences, recall the analysis propounded
in section 4.2.1 above:

> The *information contained* in a set $ of sentences in context i is the
> proposition p, such that p is the conglomerate proposition ex-
> pressed by $ in context i.

In light of our latest discussion, it is obvious that this analysis
is unsatisfactory because it fails to take into account the requirement that the information that P is present only if the message
in question originates with someone in a position to know that
P. In other words, the analysis must incorporate the requirement
that the set $ of sentences originate with someone in a position
to know that P.

The notion of a set of sentences "originating with someone"
needs explication, however. For a set of sentences (or sentence
types) is a set of abstract entities existing regardless of the activities, or even the existence, of any informant. Hence the sense
in which a set of sentences "originates" with an individual must
be made clear.

Let us consider an example involving a text containing some
information. Suppose Jones is an amateur meteorologist. Jones
keeps a log book in which he records, each day, various weather

conditions as measured by his instruments. Suppose that on June 4, 1980 Jones makes the following entry in his log:

> The high temperature today was eighty-two degrees, the low fifty-six degrees. There was no precipitation. There were high cumulus clouds all day.

These sentences contain information. As noted in Chapter 4, *what* information they contain is a function of the context in which they (or, more precisely, their tokens) appear. For the same entry made in another part of the log book may contain different information. But furthermore, *that* these sentences contain information also depends on the context in which they (or, again, their tokens) appear. For the same entry made by someone *not in a position to know* the high and low temperatures of the day, the precipitation, and the nature of the clouds would not contain this information. Hence, not only *what* information is contained in a set of sentences, but *whether* information is contained in a set of sentences, depends on context.

Generalizing from this example, we may state that a set $ of sentences expressing the proposition p in context i contains the information that P only if the agent who produces tokens of the elements of $ in context i is in a position to know that P. Hence, in the case of containing information, the notion of a set of sentences "originating with someone" has to do with the agent who produces tokens of the sentences in the set in question, in the appropriate context. Consequently, the change required to bring the above analysis of 'information contained' in line with our findings about being in a position to know is to specify that the agent who produces tokens of the sentences in the set in question, in context i, be in a position to know the proposition expressed by the set of sentences in context i.

Reference to the agent in question, we may suppose, is already part of any index i describing a context. For recall from our earlier discussion of contexts and indices (in section 4.1.4) that among the co-ordinates included in an index is a *speaker co-ordinate* (which should be understood as referring to the agent who produces tokens of the sentences in question, whether this production is verbal or written). Thus the agent in question is already part of any context we may discuss. Let us call the individual designated by the speaker co-ordinate of index i the *agent of the context* designated by i.

With the help of this terminology, we may state the amended version of our analysis of the information contained by a group of sentences as follows:

> The *information* (if any) *contained* in a set $ of sentences in context i is the proposition p, such that
> 1. p is the conglomerate proposition expressed by $ in context i,
> 2. the agent of context i is in a position to know that P.

The addition of the parenthetical "if any" in the above analysis is made necessary by the possibility that the agent of the context is not in a position to know p at all—in this case the sentences contain no information.

It may be objected that the requirement that the agent of the context be in a position to know the conglomerate proposition p expressed by $ is too strict. This objection can be illustrated with an example. Let us consider Jones the amateur meteorologist again. Imagine that Jones makes the same entry as before in his log book, only now suppose that part of his entry is a guess. Jones' machine for measuring the daily high and low temperatures breaks down, so that it only reliably measures the high temperature and not the low. Since Jones is a stickler for completeness (and much less of a stickler for accuracy), he guesses the low temperature for the day and enters it in his log book.

Now the conglomerate proposition expressed by Jones' entry represents the world as being such that the high temperature is 82 degrees, the low is 56 degrees, the precipitation is 0, and the clouds are high cumulus. However, since Jones is not in a position to know that the low temperature is 56 degrees, he is not in a position to know the conglomerate proposition expressed by his entire entry, either. Hence on the above analysis, Jones' entry contains *no* information. But surely this is incorrect—Jones' entry contains information about the high temperature, the precipitation, and the clouds, even though it admittedly fails to contain information about the low temperature. Thus the requirement that the agent of the context be in a position to know the conglomerate proposition expressed by the *entire* set in question is too harsh.

This objection is well taken, and it prompts a change in the analysis to allow for the possibility that the agent of the context is in a position to know the conglomerate proposition expressed by only a *part* of the set of sentences under consideration. Hence the final revision of the analysis is the following:

> The *information* (if any) *contained* in a set $ of sentences in context i is the proposition p, where
> 1. $' is the largest subset of $ such that the agent of context i is in a position to know the proposition expressed by each element of $' in context i,
> 2. p is the conglomerate proposition expressed by $' in context i.

Of course the information contained in the set $' is only that part of the conglomerate proposition that the agent of the context is in a position to know. Hence it still may be that a given set of sentences contains no information because the set $' is the empty set.

9.5.2 Information Transferred

Having revised the analysis of 'information contained' from Chapter 4 to include the requirement that the originator of the sentences in question be in a position to know, it is now a simple matter to make a like revision of our analysis of 'information transferred.' Recall that this analysis, as formulated in section 4.2.2, is as follows:

> The *information* (if any) *transferred* to Y by a set $ of sentences in context i is the proposition p if
> 1. $ is presented to Y in context i,
> 2. $' is the subset of Y consisting of only those sentences in $ heard and understood by Y,
> 3. p is the conglomerate proposition expressed by $' in context i.

In light of the results of the last section, it is clear that only clause 2 of this analysis must be changed. Furthermore, the change required is that the sentences in the set $' must not only be heard and understood by Y, they must also express propositions that the agent of the context is in a position to know. Hence the revised version of our analysis of the notion of the information transferred by a set of sentences is the following:

The *information* (if any) *transferred* to Y by a set $ of sentences in context i is the proposition p if
  1. $ is presented to Y in context i,
  2. $' is the largest subset of $ such that
     (a) the agent of context i is in a position to know every proposition expressed by some element of $' in context i,
     (b) Y hears and understands the sentences of $',
  3. p is the conglomerate proposition expressed by $' in context i.

If no sentence in $ satisfies clause 2, then $' will be empty and no information is transferred to Y by $.

It should be pointed out that there is a close connection between the above analysis of the notion of the information transferred by a set of sentences and our final analysis, in Chapter 8, of informing. In both cases it is required that the agent X of a context i send a set $ of sentences to some individual Y who receives and understands the sentences of $, and furthermore that X be in a position to know the conglomerate proposition p expressed by $ in context i. Hence we may conclude that

X informs Y that P by way of $ in context i just in case p is the information transferred to Y by $ in context i with agent X.

Less formally, we conclude that when X informs Y that P, p is the information transferred to Y by the sentences X uses in the communication. Thus the above statement is really a refinement of the Linking Principle postulated in the beginning of this chapter. In fact we have now arrived at the most precise formulation generated in this study of the relationship between informing and information.

Thus we see that the notion of the information transferred by a set of sentences is not an artificial construct produced to play a mediating role between the more crucial notions of the information contained and the information conveyed by a set of sentences. Instead, the information transferred plays a central role as the concept that links our refined versions of the propositional analysis of information to our analysis of informing.

9.5.3 Information Conveyed

The analysis of 'information conveyed' established in section 4.2.3 is as follows:

> The *information* (if any) *conveyed* to Y by the set $ of sentences in context i is the proposition p such that
> 1. there exists information q transferred to Y by $ in context i,
> 2. Y comes to believe p by virtue of the information q.

An implicit emendation of this analysis has already been carried out by virtue of the fact that the analysis of the notion of the information transferred by a set of sentences was altered in the last section. Since this change incorporates our finding that information must originate with someone in a position to know, it may appear that no further change is required. Indeed, the first clause of the above analysis is adequate as it stands thanks to this implicit change. However, it turns out that the analysis must be extended to account for a further condition associated with being in a position to know; in the case of conveying information, the *receiver* of the information that P must be in a position to know that P.

This result is rather unexpected; however a simple example serves to show that this change is necessary. Suppose that Jones *knows* that Smith intends to go to a movie or a play on Friday evening. Imagine that Smith tells Jones that he has decided not to go to a movie on Friday, from which Jones concludes that Smith intends to go to a play. According to both our intuitions and the analysis above, Smith's remark conveys to Jones the information that Smith intends to go to a play on Friday evening. In this case, all is as it should be.

In contrast, suppose that Jones does *not* have any knowledge about Smith's intentions for Friday evening, so that Jones does not know that Smith intends to go to either a play or a movie.

Suppose that Smith remarks to Jones that he has decided against going to a movie on Friday, and that from this Jones comes to believe (for whatever reason) that Smith intends to go to a play. I think it is clear that, in this case, Smith's remark does *not* convey to Jones the information that Smith intends to go to a play. Jones may have a hunch or a guess about Smith's intentions, but not the information in question. However, note that according to the analysis of information conveyed stated above, Smith's remark *does* convey this information to Jones. Thus the above analysis is inadequate.

In comparing these two examples, it seems clear that the crucial factor determining whether Smith's remark conveys the information that Smith intends to go to the play is whether Jones is *in a position to know* whether Smith intends to go to the play, given Smith's remark. In the first case, Jones' prior knowledge of Smith's intentions provides justification, given Smith's remark, for Jones' belief that Smith intends to go to a play. In the second case, Jones has no evidential basis for his belief, and so he doesn't have the information in question.

In light of this counter-example, we can amend our analysis by tacking on a clause to insure that the receiver of the information conveyed by a set of sentences is in the appropriate position to know:

> The *information* (if any) *conveyed* to Y by the set $ of sentences in context i is the proposition p such that
>   1. there exists information q transferred to Y by $ in context i,
>   2. Y comes to believe p by virtue of q,
>   3. Y is in a position to know p, given q.

It should be noted that the looseness of the connection between transferring information and conveying information is increased by this change. It was already the case that quite a gulf separated these notions as a result of the requirement that the receiver of information have certain beliefs in the latter case, while there was no such requirement in the former. This gulf has now widened because of the further condition, in the latter case, that the receiver of information be in an appropriate position to know, which is not required in the former case.

Thus it may happen that a set $ of sentences sent from X to Y may convey the information that P to Y when X does not believe that P, and perhaps is not even in a position to know that P. But of course this aspect of our account only mirrors everyday occurrences along these lines (as indeed it must). For example, suppose that Jones knows that Q obtains only if P obtains, but knows nothing about whether P or Q obtain. On the other hand, Smith may know that Q obtains, but be ignorant of the fact that Q only if P. If Smith informs Jones that Q, then, assuming Jones draws the obvious conclusion, Smith's statement that Q conveys the information that P to Jones. Yet Smith doesn't believe that P and Smith is not in a position to know that P. Nevertheless, our intuitions suggest (and the analysis agrees) that Smith's remark does convey to Jones the information that P.

In conclusion, it may seem rather odd that the condition of being in a position to know, which all along has been required of the *originator* of information and of the *informant* in an act of informing, should suddenly be required of the *receiver* of the information conveyed by a set of sentences. However a coherent view of the entire picture is available if we introduce an ordinary language notion that we have up to now not mentioned: the notion of *having*, or *being in the possession of, information*. The next subsection makes use of this notion to draw together the several discussions involving being in a position to know which are spread over this and the previous chapter.

9.5.4 Having Information

A position regarding what counts as having the information that P is a straightforward consequence of our analysis of informing and an apparently indisputable principle regarding the connection between having information and informing. The principle in question is the following:

X informs Y that P only if X has the information that P.

In other words, one can only inform someone that P when one *has* the information that P—one cannot pass along information that one doesn't have. Thus having the information that P is a necessary (though obviously not a sufficient) condition of informing someone that P. Since our analysis of informing specifies necessary and sufficient conditions for informing someone that P, we need only consider the conditions set forth in this analysis to arrive at an analysis of having the information that P.

The analysis of 'inform' stated at the end of Chapter 8 is the following:

X informs Y that P if
1. There exists a set $ of sentences such that
   (a) X sends $ to Y in context i,
   (b) Y receives and understands the sentences of $,
   (c) p is the conglomerate proposition expressed by $ in context i,
2. X is in a position to know that P.

Regarding clause 1 of this explication, it is immediately clear that it does not constitute, and is not necessary for, having the information that P. For one may have the information that P without ever telling anyone that P, or even saying that P. For example, suppose that Jones finds out that his neighbor is an alcoholic, but decides to keep it under his hat, and does. Then Jones has the information that his neighbor is an alcoholic, even though Jones never utters or writes any sentence tokens to this effect. Thus we may dismiss clause 1 as being irrelevant to whether X has the information that P.

This leaves clause 2, suggesting that X has the information that P just in case X is in a position to know that P. Although this will be our eventual conclusion, there is one obvious objection to this position that must be addressed. It might be suggested that having the information that P cannot be a "passive" sort of thing—one must at least *believe* that P in order to have the information that P.

I offer two arguments in reply to this objection. The first is an indirect argument based on the principle linking informing with having information. Suppose that X has the information that P only if X believes that P. Then since X can inform Y that P only if X has the information that P, it follows from the principle of hypothetical syllogism that X can inform Y that P only if X believes that P. However we have seen (in Chapter 7) that an informant need not believe that P in order to inform another that P, so this last conditional is false. It follows that our original assumption (that X has the information that P only if X believes that P) is false.

The second argument is based directly on ordinary use, and consists of a counter-example to the claim in question. Suppose that Jones' friend Smith moves into an apartment recently vacated by Jones' friend Scott. Suppose that Jones knows that Smith took over Scott's utility and phone accounts (so that Smith's new telephone number is Scott's old telephone number) and that Jones knows Scott's old phone number. Imagine that one day Jones decides to call Smith for the first time at his new abode. Having failed to put two and two together, Jones calls directory assistance to obtain Smith's new number (and is suitably embarrassed when he recognizes Scott's old number). It seems perfectly legitimate to describe this situation as one in which Jones *had* the information that Smith's phone number was so-and-so, but failed to realize it, and indeed did not believe (for awhile) that it was so-and-so.

Certainly there are scads of like counter-examples. Empirical researchers often have data which, when properly interpreted, will yield the information that P, yet the researcher fails to realize this and hence fails to believe that P despite having the information that P. And of course there are (too many) examples in everyday life like the one above, in which a failure to draw a simple conclusion deprives one of the belief that P despite one's possession of the information that P. Hence I conclude that believing that P is not necessary for having the information that P.

Despite the possibility that X may have the information that P without believing that P, X must be in a position to know that P in order to have the information that P. It should be noted that this assertion is borne out in the examples above. Hence to complete the argument begun at the beginning of the subsection, we need only conclude that being in a position to know is both the necessary and the sufficient condition for having information. More formally,

X *has the information* that P if X is in a position to know that P.

It should now of course be possible to replace all references to being in a position to know that P in the discussion above with references to having the information that P, if we wish.

With this in mind, we can now reconsider the relationship between those analyses above that make use of the notion of being in a position to know. As already noted, an informant obviously must have the information that P in order to inform someone that P. Likewise, it seems clear that if some text contains the information that P, then the person who originated the text must have had the information that P. Similarly for the information transferred by a text, which is so closely related to informing. In all these cases, it is required that the originator of a message carrying the information that P have the information that P "to put into the message," so to speak. However, these notions do not require that a receiver (if any) of the messages involved themselves get (i.e., come to have) the information carried by the message, or any other information. However, in the case of *conveying* information, it *is* necessary that the recipient of the message get some information as a result of receiving the message. Hence the requirement that the receiver of a message have the information that P (i.e., be in a position to know that P) is required in the analysis of this last notion. When viewed in this light, the analysis of 'information conveyed' is seen to cohere well with the other analyses provided in this study.

In closing this discussion, it should be noted that all the conclusions about the information contained in, transferred by, and conveyed by a set of sentences, and about having information established in the last several sections can of course be extended to corresponding conclusions about misinformation by adding the stipulation that the proposition involved be false.

9.6 CONCLUSION

In this chapter many results about the nature of informing and misinforming have been extended into conclusions about the nature of information and misinformation and blended with preliminary versions of the propositional analysis to arrive at final analyses of the notions of the information (and misinformation) contained in, transferred by, and conveyed by sets of sentences. We have found that: information need not be true, though misinformation must be false; information need not be believed by anyone; information need not originate with a reliable informant, but it must originate with someone in an appropriate position to know.

Ontologically, information is propositions, but which proposition comprises the information carried by a given set of sentences depends upon contextual factors, and whether one's concern is with the information contained in, transferred by, or conveyed by the set of sentences.

With this chapter, the main tasks of this study have been completed. To recall section 1.1.5, it was stated that one of the primary concerns of the work was to determine as exactly and clearly as possible what sort of thing information is. The propositional analysis of information, particularly in its elaboration in terms of the analyses of 'information contained', 'information transferred', and 'information conveyed' realizes this goal.

Another goal of this investigation was to examine the process of informing. This goal is realized in the discussion carried out in Chapters 5 through 8, culminating in the analysis of 'inform' propounded at the end of Chapter 8.

Finally, it was stated that a concern of the study would be to investigate the two companion notions to information and informing, misinformation and misinforming. This aim has also been achieved by supplying conclusions and analyses concerning misinforming and misinformation to accompany all major conclusions and analyses established in the essay concerning informing and information.

Therefore, as stated, the major goals of this essay have now been achieved. As is always the case, however, important and difficult questions about information and its cognate notions remain. For example the extremely troublesome but practically crucial notion of the *amount* of information carried by a set of sentences remains unanalyzed. The notion of *informativeness* remains unanalyzed.

Furthermore, it is clear that several aspects of the account presented in this work are in need of further investigation. The notion of being in a position to know is surrounded with subtle difficulties. The details of how meaning determines propositional content as a function of context is not well understood. Finally, a better understanding of the nature of propositions is required if we are to fully understand information.

All of these remaining problems are very difficult, and each demands a large-scale investigation for its successful resolution. Consequently this essay must be regarded as only the first step toward a complete theory of information for information science.

BIBLIOGRAPHY

Artandi, S., "Information Concepts and Their Utility," *Journal of the ASIS* 24 (1973):242–245.

Austin, J. L., "A Plea for Excuses," in C. Lyas (ed.), *Philosophy and Linguistics*, London: Macmillan, 1971, 79–101.

_____, *How To Do Things With Words*, Cambridge: Harvard University Press, 1975.

Bar-Hillel, Yehoshua, "A Logician's Reaction to Recent Theorizing on Information Search Systems," *American Documentation* 8 (1957):103–113.

_____, *Language and Information*, Reading, Mass.: Addison-Wesley, 1964.

Barnes, R. F., "Information and Decision," in A. Debons and W. A. Cameron (eds.), *Perspectives in Information Science*, Leydon: Noordof, 1975, 105–117.

Belkin, N. J., "Information Concepts for Information Science," *Journal of Documentation* 34 (1978):55–85.

_____, "Some Soviet Concepts of Information for Information Science," *Journal of the ASIS* 26 (1975):56–64.

_____, "Towards a Definition of Information for Informatics," *Informatics* 2 (1974):50–56.

Belkin, N. J. and S. E. Robertson, "Information Science and the Phenomenon of Information," *Journal of the ASIS* 27 (1976):197–210.

Bettinger, Ross J., "Letter to the ACM Forum," *Communications of the ACM* 24 #7 (1981), 281.

Boulding, Kenneth E., *The Image: Knowledge in Life and Society*, Ann Arbor: University of Michigan Press, 1956.

Brookes, B. C., "The Fundamental Problem of Information Science," in V. Horsnell (ed.), *Informatics* 2, London: Aslib, 1975, 42–49.

Carnap, Rudolph and Yehoshua Bar-Hillel, "An Outline of a Theory of Semantic Information," Technical Report 247 of the Research Laboratory of Electronics, Massachusetts Institute of Technology, 1952.

Cartwright, Richard, "Propositions," in Ronald Butler (ed.), *Analytic Philosophy*, New York: Barnes and Noble, 1962, 81–103.

Davidson, Donald and Gilbert Harmon, (eds.), *The Logic of Grammar*, Encino, Calif: Dickenson Publishing Co., 1975.

———— (eds.), *Semantics of Natural Language*, Boston: Reidel, 1972.

Debons, A., *Determining Information Functions*, Discussion Paper, NSF Manpower Survey Project DS1-7727115, November, 1978.

Dow, J. T., "A Metatheory for the Development of a Science of Information," *Journal of the ASIS* 28 (1977):323–331.

Dretske, Fred, *Knowledge and the Flow of Information*, Cambridge: The MIT Press, 1981.

Fairthorne, R. A., "Information: One Label, Several Bottles," in A. Debons and W. J. Cameron (eds.), *Perspectives in Information Science*, Leyden: Noordhof, 1975, 65–73.

————, "The Morphology of Information Flow," *Journal of the ACM* 14 (1967):710–719.

————, " 'Use' and 'Mention' in the Information Sciences," in Laurence Heilprin (ed.), *Proceedings of the Symposium on Education for Information Science*, Washington: Spartan Books, 1965.

Farradane, J., "The Nature of Information," *Journal of Information Science Principles and Practices* 1 (1979):13–18.

————, "Towards a True Information Science," *The Information Scientist* 10 (1976):91–101.

Filmore, Ch., "Entailment Rules in a Semantic Theory," in Rosenberg and Travis (eds.), *Readings in Philosophy of Language*, New York: Prentice Hall, 1971, 533–547.

Gorovitz, Samuel, Merrill Hintikka, Donald Provence, and Ron G. Williams, *Philosophical Analysis*, New York: Random House, 1979.

Grice, H. P., "Logic and Conversation," in Donald Davidson and Gilbert Harmon (eds.), *The Logic of Grammar*, Encino, Calif: Dickenson Publishing Co., 1975, 64–74.

Jones, D. S., *Elementary Information Theory*, Oxford: The Clarendon Press, 1979.

Kaplan, David, "On the Logic of Demonstratives," *Journal of Philosophical Logic* 8 (1979):81–98.

Karttunen, L., "Some Observations on Factivity," *Papers in Linguistics* 4 (1972):55–70.

Katz, J. J., *Semantic Theory*, New York: Harper and Row, 1972.

Keenan, E., "Presupposition in Natural Logic," *Monist* 57,3 (1973).

Kiparsky, P. and C. Kiparsky, "Fact," in D. Steinberg and L. Jakobovits (eds.), *Semantics: An Interdisciplinary Reader in Philosophy, Linguistics and Psychology*, London: Cambridge University Press, 1971, 345–369.

Kripke, Saul, "Speaker's Reference and Semantic Reference," in Peter French, Theodore Uhling Jr., and Howard Wettstein, (eds.), *Midwest Studies in Philosophy*, Volume 2, Morris: University of Minnesota Press, 1977, 255–276.

Lehrer, Keith, *Knowledge*, Oxford: The Clarendon Press, 1974.

Lewis, David, "General Semantics," in Donald Davidson and Gilbert Harmon, (eds.), *Semantics of Natural Language*, Boston: Reidel, 1972, 169–218.

Lyas, Colin, (ed.), *Philosophy and Linguistics*, London: Macmillan, 1971.

Maxwell, Grover and Herbert Feigl, "Why Ordinary Language Needs Reforming," in Richard Rorty (ed.), *The Linguistic Turn*, Chicago: University of Chicago Press, 1967, 193–200.

Otten, K., "Basis for a Science of Information," in A. Debons (ed.) *Information Science: Search for Identity*, New York: Marcel Dekker, 1974, 91–106.

Otten, K. and A. Debons, "Toward a Metascience of Information: Informatology," *Journal of the ASIS* 21 (1970):89–94.

Oxford English Dictionary, Volume 5, Oxford: The Clarendon Press, 1933.

Pelletier, F. J., "On Some Proposals for the Semantics of Mass Nouns," *Journal of Philosophical Logic* 3 (1974):87–108.

Pratt, A. D., "An Essay on the Nature of Information," *Proceedings of the American Documentation Institute*, Volume 4, Washington: Thompson Book Co., 1967, 3–5.

_____, "The Information of the Image," *Libri* 27 (1977):204–220.

Quine, W. V., *From a Logical Point of View*, New York: Harper and Row, 1961.

_____, *Word and Object*, Cambridge: The M.I.T. Press, 1960.

Rapoport, A., "What is Information?," in Tefco Saracevic (ed.), *Introduction to Information Science*, New York: Bowker, 1970, 5–12.

Rathswohl, E. J., "Tutorial, Group I: The Nature of Information," in A. Debons and W. J. Cameron (eds.), *Perspectives in Information Science*, Leyden: Noordhof, 1975, 21–30.

Rorty, Richard (ed.), *The Linguistic Turn*, Chicago: University of Chicago Press, 1967.

Ryle, G., "Use and Usage," in C. Lyas (ed.), *Philosophy and Linguistics*, London: Macmillan, 1971, 45–60.

Salmon, Wesley, *Logic*, Englewood Cliffs: Prentice-Hall, 1973.

Samuelson, K., "Information Models and Theories—A Synthesizing Approach," in A. Debons (ed.), *Information Science: Search for Identity*, New York: Marcel Dekker, 1974, 47–67.

Saracevic, Tefco, (ed.), *Introduction to Information Science*, New York: Bowker, 1970.

Schlick, Moritz, "The Future of Philosophy," in Richard Rorty (ed.), *The Linguistic Turn*, Chicago: University of Chicago Press, 1967, 43–53.

Schreider, Yu A., "On the Semantic Characteristics of Information," *Information Storage and Retrieval* 3 (1965):221–233.

Searle, J. R., "The Background of Meaning," in J. R. Searle, F. Kiefer, and M. Bierwisch (eds.), *Speech Act Theory and Pragmatics*, Boston: Reidel, 1980, 221–231.

Shannon, C. E., "A Mathematical Theory of Communication," *Bell System Technical Journal* 27 (1948): 379–423.

Shannon, C. E. and W. Weaver, *The Mathematical Theory of Communication*, Chicago: University of Illinois Press, 1949.

Stalnaker, Robert, "Assertion," in Peter Cole (ed.), *Syntax and Semantics*, V. 9; *Pragmatics*, New York: Academic Press, 1978, 315–332.

———, "Pragmatics," in Donald Davidson and Gilbert Harmon, (eds.), *Semantics of Natural Language*, Boston: Reidel, 1972, 380–397.

Steinberg, Danny D. and Leon A. Jakobovits, (eds.), *Semantics: An Interdisciplinary Reader in Philosophy, Linguistics and Psychology*, London: Cambridge University Press, 1971.

Wellisch, H., "From Information Science to Informatics: A Terminological Investigation," *Journal of Librarianship* 4 (1972):157–187.

Wersig, Gernot and Ulrich Neveling, "The Phenomena of Interest to Information Science," *The Information Scientist* 9 (1975):127–140.

Whittemore, B. J. and M. C. Yovits, "A Generalized Concept for the Analysis of Information," in A. Debons (ed.), *Information Science: Search for Identity*, New York: Marcel Dekker, 1974, 29–45.

———, "A Generalized Conceptual Development for the Analysis and Flow of Information," *Journal of the ASIS* 24 (1973):221–231.

Wilson, Deirdre, "Presupposition on Factives," *Linguistic Inquiry* 3 (1972).

Wilson, P., "Some Fundamental Concepts of Information Retrieval," *Drexel Library Quarterly* 14 #2 (1978):10–24.

Yovits, M. C. and R. L. Ernst, "Generalized Information Systems," in A. Kent (ed.), *Electronic Handling of Information: Testing and Evaluation*, Washington: Thompson, 1967, 279–290.

INDEX

About the Author

CHRISTOPHER FOX received his Ph.D. from the School of Information Studies at Syracuse University. He is presently Assistant Professor of Computer Science at Bowling Green State University in Ohio.